A Practical Guide to Service Learning

Felicia L. Wilczenski and Susan M. Coomey

A Practical Guide to Service Learning

Strategies for Positive Development in Schools

 Springer

Felicia L. Wilczenski
Graduate College of Education
Dept. of Counseling & School Psychology
University of Massachusetts
100 Morrissey Blvd.
Boston, MA 02125
USA
Felicia.Wilczenski@umb.edu

Susan M. Coomey
Wachusett Regional High School
1401 Main Street
Holden, MA 01520
USA
Susan_Coomey@wrsd.net

Library of Congress Control Number: 2006937531

ISBN-10: 0-387-46538-3   e-ISBN-10: 0-387-46540-5
ISBN-13: 978-0-387-46538-8   e-ISBN-13: 978-0-387-46540-1

Printed on acid-free paper.

9 8 7 6 5 4 3 2 1

springer.com

This book is dedicated in memory of my parents, Louis and Genevieve Wilczenski, who set an example of kindness and generosity that remains my measure. FLW

I dedicate this book to my parents, John and Rose Higgins, who taught me that service and learning are integral to life, and to my husband Michael, son Joshua, and daughter Sarah, for their ongoing and invaluable support. SMC

Preface

"School is so *boring*! I *hate* it!" "Why do I have to learn this stuff? I'll never use it!" "What does this class have to do with *anything*?" As school psychologists and school counselors, how often do you hear this? Chances are many of the students referred to you do not have any cognitive impairment or emotional disability. They are bored and disengaged from school. Some students may be struggling with personal and career identity issues. Others come to you when interpersonal concerns or emotional distress interfere with their ability to learn. Still others have learning disabilities, cognitive impairment, or psychological disorders that hinder their academic progress. In this era of standards-based instruction and *No Child Left Behind,* the bottom line for schools is students' academic performance. The intense pressure on teachers to close the achievement gap and to produce students who achieve academically also pressures you to find effective interventions to promote school success. Ultimately, the goal of your work is to enable academic learning to take place—for both regular and special education students. The challenge is enormous.

Traditional counseling practices in schools can fall short in answering that challenge. For example, you may find yourself frustrated trying to help students generalize the social skills, conflict resolution strategies, and coping mechanisms that you have role-played or discussed with students during counseling sessions to the "real world" outside your office. It is often difficult for students to apply the insights and skills they learn through counseling to other settings and situations, and therefore, easy to see that interpersonal skills and emotional regulation are more likely to be developed when people interact with one another in real-world contexts. Traditional methods are often not effective in motivating disengaged students who have little support or encouragement regarding their education and see no reason to come to school. Furthermore, the traditional organizational structures found in schools today can restrict you to working with students outside of their classrooms or to developing academic interventions that are applied in isolation within a classroom, without integrating the information in any context or relating it to other areas of study.

We know both intuitively and through research that people learn best by doing and reflecting on what they have done. How often have you sat in a professional development meeting looking at your watch, bored and disengaged, listening to a speaker drone on about something job-related that you are required to know? You are exposed to the information, but you are not really absorbing it. You may find that it is only when you are on the job, applying the information yourself, using it, living it, reflecting on it, that you truly understand and make sense of it and will remember it. You did not learn how to counsel students or give a cognitive test by reading about it or listening to a lecture on it. Certainly those were necessary means of learning about counseling and test administration. Your real learning began the day you began doing it and reflecting on what you did. Students are no different—they need active engagement to acquire information and to grapple with complex social issues while being immersed in a stimulating learning context. They need to think about and process those experiences.

This book introduces school-based mental health professionals to service learning as an evidence-based intervention. Service learning is an experiential approach to education that involves students in meaningful, real-world activities that can advance social, emotional, career, and academic curricula goals while benefiting communities. We realized the potential of service learning to enhance school psychology and school counseling practices when we observed the positive impact of service-learning experiences for our own students in graduate school and in K-12 settings. In essence, service learning is social, emotional, career, and academic education in action.

School psychologists and other school-based mental health professionals are constantly seeking interventions that can positively affect social/emotional as well as career and academic outcomes. Increasingly, teachers and administrators recognize that social, emotional, and career learning should be an integral part of the academic curriculum in the schools.

Service learning can link the social, emotional, and career developmental concerns of mental health professionals with the academic mission of schools. At the same time, service learning brings academic knowledge to life through real-world learning contexts. The ability to teach social/emotional, career, and academic concepts simultaneously makes service learning one of the most powerful interventions possible.

The book is written from the perspective of school-based mental health professionals and offers guidelines and resources, informed by research, for school psychologists and counselors interested in implementing service learning. We have incorporated real-world experiences of practicing school psychologists and school counselors who have successfully employed service learning in their work. Through their experiences, service-learning applications in school psychology and school counseling come alive. Moreover, this book will offer its readers service-learning strategies that can forge critical links to join their work with the academic mission of schools. Through service learning, school-based mental health professionals have an opportunity to broaden their role to encompass both regular and special education.

As an introduction to service learning for the school-based mental health professions, the book is appropriate for practitioners and for use in professional preparation courses. It is a valuable resource for internship students in school psychology and school counseling as well as for continuing professional development. We hope that this book will help make service learning an integral part of school-based mental health practices.

Acknowledgments

We extend our sincere appreciation to the many colleagues and students who inspired us to write this book. We especially want to acknowledge University of Massachusetts Boston colleagues, Dwight Giles and John Saltmarsh, whose exemplary scholarship and teaching has significantly influenced our work, and also Rebecca Schumacher for her insightful comments and helpful suggestions. Thanks to Peter Lee of the Boston Massachusetts Public Schools for his support of the BostonNET project. Thank you to UMass Boston graduate students Amani Allen, Kenycia Byrd, Michael Houlihan, Bic Lam, Aaron McCabe, and Lori Suher for help with library research and to Rene Puopolo for sharing her experience using service learning. We are grateful to Paula Leva, Diane Johnson, and Mindy Sefton of the Shrewsbury Massachusetts Public Schools who encouraged us to implement our ideas. We want to express a special thank you to Michael Coomey for his technical assistance throughout this project. Finally, we are indebted to Springer editors Judy Jones and Angela Burke, who saw the value of infusing service learning in school psychology and school counseling practices and to Madhurima Biswas for her help in preparing the manuscript for publication.

Contents

Introduction

A Practical Guide to Service Learning: Strategies for Positive Development in Schools presents the theory and application of service learning for school psychologists and school counselors. Service learning has synergistic effects in promoting positive social and emotional growth as well as in enhancing career and academic outcomes. The graphic illustrates the dynamic interrelationship between and among social, emotional, career, and academic learning and the center circle indicates how service connects learning in the four areas.

Service learning is:

- Linkage of service to academic content and standards.
- Personal and social learning.
- Opportunities for career exploration.
- Helping to determine and meet real community needs.
- Beneficial for both the students and the community.
- Appropriate in any subject area to meet learning goals.
- Suitable for students at all grade levels.

Service learning is not:

- Sporadic volunteer programs.
- Added on to an existing curriculum.
- Logging a set number of community service hours for an award.
- Only for high school and college students.
- One-sided—benefiting only the students or only the community.

Real-world service learning is:

- Positive, meaningful, and real to the participants.
- Cooperative rather than competitive.
- Exposure to complex problems in complex settings.
- Opportunities for creative problem solving and critical thinking.
- Deeper learning because the results are immediate and uncontrived.
- Personally meaningful to participants, generating emotional consequences that challenge values as well as ideas that support social, emotional, and cognitive development (see Eyler & Giles, 1999).

Essential components of service learning:

1. Service

    A. Engaging students to act for some common good.
    B. Using the skills and energy of students to address real-life needs.

2. Learning

    A. Engaging the students in thinking about the larger issues connected to their service.
    B. Participatory or hands-on experiences.

3. Reflection

    A. The critical component of successful service-learning programs.
    B. The process of deriving meaning and knowledge from experience before, during, and after a service-learning project. Effective reflection engages students and adult facilitators in a thoughtful process that consciously connects learning with experience. It is the use of critical thinking skills to learn from service experiences and from each other.

Service Learning Is a Bridge

Why should school psychologists and school counselors incorporate service learning in their practices? Service learning can serve as a bridge to connect the work of school-based mental health professionals and educators, including teachers and administrators. School psychologists and school counselors (including guidance counselors, adjustment counselors, and school social workers) focus on the socialization processes of schooling and seek to promote students' social and emotional development. However, mental health practices in schools are frequently decontextualized and center on interventions, such as counseling, to meet the social and emotional needs of individual students. Mental health interventions, therefore, are often considered secondary to the academic mission of schools.

Service Learning Is Effective

Empirical evidence indicates that service learning is a promising practice to enhance social and emotional development and thereby fosters academic growth and resiliency among students. Service learning supports character education by giving students opportunities to be caring and helpful community members. Career exploration is also facilitated through service learning. Furthermore, service learning can forge mutually beneficial school and community partnerships.

Service-learning interventions simultaneously yield personal, social, emotional, career, and academic learning benefits, suggesting that they all have a common basis. RMC Research Corporation (2003) and the National Service-Learning Clearinghouse (2006) compiled bibliographies highlighting research findings that document the impacts and outcomes of service learning in K-12 settings (see http://servicelearning.org/lib_svcs/bibs/k-12_bibs/impacts_k-12/ and http://servicelearning.org/resources/fact_sheets/k-12_facts/why/). The following is a summary of key findings concerning service learning that are relevant to the work of school psychologists and counselors:

- *Service learning increases student engagement.* Research shows that students typically become more engaged in learning as evidenced by increased attendance and motivation to learn (e.g., Melchior, 1999; Shumer, 1994).
- *Service learning helps students improve academically.* Research findings indicate that students show gains in academic achievement, including grades and standardized tests (e.g., Civic Literacy Project, 2000; Scales, Blyth, Berkas, & Kielsmeier, 2000).
- *Service learning fosters personal and social development.* Studies show strong positive effects on character development, reduction of risk behaviors, acceptance of diversity, responsibility, trustworthiness, and caring for others (e.g., Melchior, 1999; Switzer, Simmons, Dew, Regalski, & Wang, 1995).
- *Service learning promotes career exploration.* Students come in contact with adults in various and, perhaps, unfamiliar careers, and this exposure can translate to more varied career aspirations (e.g., Billig, Jesse, Calvert, & Kleimann, 1999; Melchior, 1999).
- *Service learning reduces risk-taking behaviors.* Studies show a reduction in aggression, delinquency, and sexually risky behaviors (e.g., Allen, Kuperminc, Philliber, & Herre, 1994; Yates & Youniss, 1996).

- *Service learning is associated with positive school environments.* Research indicates that when practiced school-wide, a more caring school climate develops (e.g., Weiler, LaGoy, Crane, & Rovner, 1998).
- *Service learning helps students develop stronger attachments to school and community.* Studies suggest that students show greater bonding to school because of increased motivation to learn and also a greater sense of civic responsibility because of the observable outcomes of their work in the community (e.g., Stephens, 1995; Youniss, McLellan, & Yates, 1997).
- *Service learning engenders community support for school.* Evidence indicates that community members view students more favorably and increase volunteer as well as financial support for schools (e.g., Billig & Conrad, 1997; Melchior, 1999).

The National Service-Learning Clearinghouse database contains many bibliographies that provide useful references on a given service-learning topic, with links to online full-text items and if available, downloadable PDF files. (See http://servicelearning.org/lib_svcs/bibs/k-12_bibs/index.php?search_term=bibliographies.004.00.)

Researchers in the field of social and emotional education embrace service learning as a strategy to foster the five core social and emotional competencies: self-awareness, social awareness, self-management, relationship skills, and decision making (Collaborative for Academic, Social, and Emotional Learning, 2003; Education Commission of the States, 2003). Social and emotional learning interventions embedded in a service-learning curriculum can be designed to address both preventive and remedial goals for individual students as well as for classrooms and schools. Through service-learning opportunities within communities, social, emotional, career, and academic learning takes place in a real-world context. Moreover, many provisions of the No Child Left Behind Act of 2001 suggested that service learning be implemented as a strategy for promoting career and academic success.

Facts and Figures

The National Youth Leadership Council produced the following list of facts concerning the impact of service learning nationwide:

4:1 Monetary value of service provided by Learn and Serve student participants to their communities, compared to Learn and Serve money spent.[1]

4.7 Estimated millions of US kindergarten through 12th-grade students engaged in service-learning.[1]

28 Percentage of public schools engaged in *service-learning*, which is curriculum-based, has clear learning objectives, and meets community needs.[2]

---

[1] Melchior, Alan, (1999) "Summary Report: National Evaluation of Learn and Serve America." Center for Human Resources, Brandeis University. Available at *www.learnandserve.org/pdf/ research/lsreport.pdf.*

66   Percentage of public schools engaged in *community service* that is not curriculum-based.[2]

92   Percentage of principals from US schools with service-learning programs, who said service-learning has a positive impact on students' civic engagement.[2]

91   Percentage of those principals who said service-learning has a positive impact on personal and social development and school-community partnerships.[2]

88   Percentage of those principals who said service-learning has a positive impact on school climate and student engagement.[2]

86   Percentage of those principals who said service-learning has a positive impact on the larger communities view of youths as resources.[2]

85   Percentage of those principals who said service-learning has a positive impact on teacher satisfaction.[2]

83   Percentage of those principals who said service-learning has a positive impact on academic achievement.[2]

43   Percentage of principals from high-poverty schools that incorporate service-learning, who reported that service-learning has a *very positive* impact on academic achievement. In medium- to low-poverty schools that offer service-learning, the response came from 31% of principals.[3]

45   Percentage of US public high schools engaged in service-learning.[2]

30   Percentage of US public middle schools engaged in service-learning.[2]

22   Percentage of US public elementary schools engaged in service-learning.[2]

98   Percentage of the more than 900 Campus Compact member colleges that offer academic credit for service-learning.[4]

90   Percentage of those colleges that partner with kindergarten through 12th-grade schools.[4]

37   Percentage of US teacher-education institutions that prepare pre-service teachers for service-learning.[5]

37   Percentage of Americans familiar with the term "service-learning."[6]

90   Percentage of Americans who support service-learning in their local public schools when it is described as students using what they "are learning in schools for community projects."[6]

---

[2] Scales, Peter C. and Roehlkepartain, Eugene C. (2004) "Community Service and Service-Learning in U.S. Public Schools, 2004." National Youth Leadership Council. Available at *www.nylc.org/g2g*.

[3] Scales, Peter C. and Roehlkepartain, Eugene C. (2005) "Can Service-Learning Help Reduce the Achievement Gap?: New Research Points toward the Potential of Service-Learning for Low-Income Students," in Growing to Greatness 2005. National Youth Leadership Council. Available at *www.nylc.org/g2g*.

[4] Campus Compact's 2003 membership survey. Available at *www.compact.org/newscc/2003_Statistics.pdf*.

[5] Anderson, Jeffrey B. and Erickson, Joseph A. (2002) "Service-Learning in Teacher Education: How Are Prospective Teachers Being Prepared to Teach the New School Population." Citing a national study sponsored by the American Association of Colleges for Teacher Education and the National Service-Learning in Teacher Education Partnership.

[6] "Public Attitudes toward Education and Service-Learning." (2000) Roper-Starch Worldwide. Available at *www.learningindeed.org/tools*.

37   Number of states with service-learning policies and procedures.[7]

10   Number of states in which community service or service-learning can fulfill graduation requirements.[7]

1   Number of states requiring service-learning for graduation.

"Service-Learning by the Numbers" is excerpted from "Growing to Greatness 2006." Copyright 2006 National Youth Leadership Council. Available from the NYLC Resource Center at www.nylc.org. Reprinted with permission.

State Policies on Service Learning

As service learning becomes more prevalent, states are beginning to adopt policies that support and regulate its use. In 2001, the Education Commission for the States scanned service-learning policies across the 50 states (also see Piscatelli, 2005):

- One state (MD) requires service learning as a requirement for high school graduation.
- Six states (ID, MI, MN, NJ, NM, VT) include service learning in the state's education standards.
- Six states (MA, MN, MS, NJ, NM, VT) have policies regarding funding appropriations and the creation of service-learning programs.
- Seven states (AR, CT, DE, MN, OK, RI, WI) permit community service or service-learning to be applied to meet high school graduation requirements.
- Eight states (AR, CA, GA, ID, IL, LA, MT, UT) have rules and regulations addressing the creation and purpose of service-learning programs.
- Ten states (CA, CT, FL, IN, MI, MS, NC, SC, TN, TX) and DC encourage the use of service-learning to increase student achievement and engagement.
- Twenty-three states have no mention of service-learning in any state policy.

Service-Learning Applications for School-Based Mental Health Professionals

Through service learning, school psychologists, school counselors, and teachers working together can positively affect lives, including the social, emotional, career, and academic development of students. Service learning strengthens the academic experience of students because it more directly engages them, expects more from them, and takes them out of the classroom as passive recipients of information. In addition, it gets them actively involved in experiencing and understanding the relationships of what they study in class to issues and responsibilities outside of themselves. Perhaps service learning is effective because it connects to a student's emerging sense of individual responsibility and identity, to greater ownership for

---

[7] Piscatelli, Jennifer. (2005) "Sustaining Service-Learning and Youth Voice through Policy," in Growing to Greatness 2005. National Youth Leadership Council. Available at *www.nylc.org/g2g.*

learning, to the dispositions that make resiliency to peer pressure more likely, and to the realization of their own assumptions about the world.

Counseling in schools has shifted its focus from a responsive services approach to one that is integrally tied to student achievement (Stone & Dahir, 2006). Stone and Dahir suggested that the purpose of a counseling program in a school setting is to impart specific skills and to facilitate learning in a proactive and preventive manner to help all students achieve schools success through personal, social, career, and academic development experiences. School psychologists and counselors can now shift from the traditional individual remediation model to a proactive counseling model that emphasizes skill building rather than deficit reduction (Galassi & Akos, 2004). Service learning is now being recognized by school psychologists and counselors as a valuable strategy to achieve K-12 counseling programs goals while providing an opportunity to work closely with teachers in addressing the academic achievement gap (Stott & Jackson, 2005; Wilczenski & Coomey, 2008; Wilczenski & Schumacher, 2006). Because of its positive effects on personal and social development, service learning benefits all students, but may especially increase the engagement and motivation of students at risk for school failure. Peterson and Seligman (2004) specifically recommended service learning as an intervention to promote positive social and emotional outcomes.

Service learning is a strategy that can incorporate all the components of a comprehensive school-based mental health services. Service learning ties community service to an academic curriculum. Moreover, in addition to enhancing academic achievement, service learning fosters personal and social resiliency. It also supports career exploration and vocational development by providing students with real-world work roles and other helping experiences in the community, which underscore the values of caring and collaboration while increasing sensitivity to cultural diversity and awareness of social justice issues.

Service learning should be employed by school psychologists and counselors because it yields so many benefits simultaneously. It is a value-added approach because it assists multiple constituencies from schools and communities and delivers multiple benefits to each. Service learning:

- Extends standards-based reforms by providing authentic learning contexts.
- Helps students succeed academically.
- Contributes to the development of important personal and social skills.
- Promotes exploration of various career paths.
- Fosters positive school climates.
- Increases community support for schools.
- Encourages strong ties to school, community, and society at large.

Thus, service learning is the piece to integrate the work of teachers, school psychologists, and school counselors. It is the piece that integrates social, emotional, career, and academic goals. Service learning provides opportunities to reshape mental health practices in schools.

The goals of school psychologists and school counselors as well as those of teachers can be realized through a service-learning curriculum, and such a curriculum can foster a sense of purpose in youth. Service learning, as an intervention, can be both remedial or preventive and individual or systemic; it can enable school psychologists and counselors to align their efforts with educational reforms and expand their role by addressing the social and emotional needs of students within the academic mainstream. Service learning is connected with the positive psychology movement and the nurturing of purpose in youth.

How Will This Book Help School-Based Mental Health Professionals?

The No Child Left Behind Act of 2001 has five primary goals. The first three focus on improving the curriculum, learning, and achievement. Goals 4 and 5 consider students' personal and social development:

- Goal 1: All students will reach high standards, at a minimum attaining proficiency or better in reading/language arts and mathematics.
- Goal 2: All limited English proficient students will become proficient in English and reach high academic standards, at a minimum attaining proficiency or better in reading/language arts and mathematics.
- Goal 3: All students will be taught by highly qualified teachers.
- Goal 4: All students will be educated in learning environments that are safe, drug free, and conducive to learning.
- Goal 5: All students will graduate from high school.

School psychologists and counselors are uniquely positioned to address goals 4 and 5. Service learning can link all these goals of No Child Left Behind (NCLB) Act and tie the work of mental health professionals to the academic mission of schools. This book provides practical, well-developed, evidence-based, defensible service-learning strategies to integrate the social, emotional, and career learning goals of school psychologists and school counselors with the academic learning goals of teachers. Service learning is an integrating strategy to create comprehensive, developmental, and coordinated mental health programs in schools. This, then, is a book about how to promote knowledgeable and socially responsible children, adolescents, and adults.

The book offers school-based mental health professionals and educators a firm grounding in the philosophical, psychological, and pedagogical bases of service learning as well as a review of the research literature concerning social, emotional, career, and academic outcomes. It is suggested that school psychologists and school counselors take responsibility for initiating service-learning programs or that they forge connections with ongoing service-learning projects in schools to address the social and emotional learning needs of students. Service-learning experiences provide a framework to meet social, emotional, and academic learning goals for all students. Career exploration and vocational development also can be enhanced through service-learning activities. The examples provided in this book will illustrate empirically supported service-learning interventions that can be used by school-based mental health professionals to address social and emotional issues in K-12 settings and explain how social and emotional learning can be directly linked to the academic curriculum of the school. Strategies will be recommended for assessing the impact of service-learning interventions and curriculum. Also highlighted are opportunities for linking service learning and the various academic initiatives of NCLB. This orientation is compatible with current school reforms that emphasize systemic, problem-solving, and outcomes-based models of educational practice.

This book presents the essential elements underlying service-learning program development, implementation, and evaluation in a straightforward, practical manner. It is written from the perspective of school psychologists and school counselors who can incorporate service learning as a tool to accomplish their goals. Graduate and postgraduate training is also addressed to support the ability and inclination of school-based school psychologists and counselors to integrate effective service learning in their work. We ask that you think about your current efforts to promote social, emotional, career, and academic competencies in all students and to consider how service learning can be applied in your work.

Section I provides an overview of service learning and describes best practices. Implementation issues and change processes as well as the need for professional education and development are addressed.

Section II considers service learning as intervention and prevention for the challenges faced by school-based mental health professionals.

Section III includes a service-learning blueprint with specific examples of its potential in increasing developmental assets and enhancing the work of school psychologists and counselors.

Section IV lists useful service-learning print and web resources.

References

Allen, J.P., Kuperminc, S., Philliber, S., & Herre, K. (1994). Programmatic prevention of adolescent problem behaviors: The role of autonomy, relatedness, and volunteer service in the teen outreach program. *Journal of Community Psychology*, 22, 617–638.

Billig, S., & Conrad, J. (1997). *An evaluation of the New Hampshire service-learning and educational reform project.* Denver, CO: RMC Research Corporation.

Billig, S., Jesse, D., Calvert, L., & Kleimann, K. (1999). *An evaluation of Jefferson County school district's school-to-career partnership program.* Denver, CO: RMC Research Corporation.

Civic Literacy Project. (February, 2000). *Standardized test scores improve with service-learning.* Bloomington, IN: Author.

Collaborative for Academic, Social, and Emotional Learning. (2003). *Safe and sound: An educational leader's guide to evidence-based social and emotional learning programs.* Chicago: University of Illinois.

Education Commission of the States. (March, 2001). *Service-learning policy scan.* Denver, CO: Author. Retrieved June 29, 2006, from http://www.ecs.org/clearinghouse/23/77/2377.htm.

Education Commission of the States. (2003). *Making the case for social and emotional learning and service-learning.* Denver, CO: Author.

Eyler, J., & Giles, D.E. (1999). *Where's the learning in service-learning?* San Francisco, CA: Jossey-Bass.

Galassi, J., & Akos, P. (2004). Developmental advocacy: Twenty-first century school counseling. *Journal of Counseling and Development, 82,* 146–157.

Melchior, A. (1999). *Summary report: National evaluation of Learn and Serve America.* Waltham, MA: Center for Human Resources, Brandeis University.

National Service-Learning Clearinghouse. (February, 2006). *Impacts and outcomes of service-learning: K-12 selected resources.* Scotts Valley, CA: Author. Retrieved June 5, 2006, from http://servicelearning.org/lib_svcs/bibs/k-12_bibs/impacts_k-12/.

No Child Left Behind Act. of (2001). Pub. L. No. 107–110.

Peterson, C., & Seligman, M.E.P. (2004). *Character strengths and virtues: A handbook and classification.* New York: Oxford University Press and Washington, DC: American Psychological Association.

Piscatelli, J. (2005). Sustaining service-learning and youth voice through policy. In *Growing to greatness: The state of service-learning project* (pp. 59–60). St. Paul, MN: National Youth Leadership Council.

RMC Research Corporation. (January, 2003*). Why districts, schools, and classrooms should practice service-learning.* Denver, CO: Author. Retrieved June 5, 2006, from http://servicelearning.org/resources/fact_sheets/k-12_facts/why/.

Scales, P., Blyth, D., Berkas, T., & Kielsmeier, J. (2000). The effects of service-learning on middle school students' social responsibility and academic success. *Journal of Early Adolescence, 20,* 331–358.

Shumer, R. (1994). Community-based learning: Humanizing education. *Journal of Adolescence, 17,* 357–367.

Stephens, L. (1995). *The complete guide to learning through community service, grades K-9.* Boston, MA: Allyn & Bacon.

Stone, C.B., & Dahir, C.A. (2006). *The transformed school counselor.* Boston, MA: Lahaska Press.

Stott, K.A., & Jackson, A.P. (2005). Using service-learning to achieve middle school comprehensive guidance program goals. *Professional School Counseling, 9,* 156–159.

Switzer, G., Simmons, R., Dew, M., Regalski, J., & Wang, C. (1995). The effect of a school-based helper program on adolescent self-image, attitudes, and behavior. *Journal of Early Adolescence, 15,* 429–455.

Weiler, D., LaGoy, A., Crane, E., & Rovner, A. (1998). *An evaluation of K-12 service-learning in California: Phase II final report.* Emeryville, CA: RPP International with the Search Institute.

Wilczenski, F.L., & Coomey, S.M. (in press, 2008). Best practices in service-learning: Enhancing both the social/emotional and academic competence of all students. In Thomas & J. Grimes (Eds.), *Best practices in school psychology—V.* Bethesda, MD: National Association of School Psychologists.

Wilczenski, F.L., & Schumacher, R.A. (2006). Giving and growing: Service-learning applications in school counseling. *School Counselor, 43(4),* 58–63.

Yates, M., & Youniss, J. (1996). A developmental perspective on community service in adolescence. *Journal of Social Issues, 54,* 495–512.

Youniss, J., McLellan, I.A., & Yates, M. (1997). What we know about engendering civic identity. *American Behavioral Scientist, 40,* 620–631.

Section I
Service Learning for School Psychologists and School Counselors

Social, emotional, career, and academic learning take place at school. Traditionally, they are treated as discrete entities, as disconnected pieces of a puzzle:

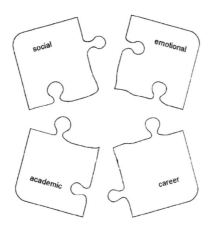

Service learning provides the context to connect social, emotional, career, and academic learning:

Even though there are clear connections between service-learning and positive social, emotional, career, and academic outcomes, service learning has not been a prominent feature in the work of mental health professionals in schools. Yet, social, emotional, and career development is within the purview of school psychologists and counselors, and community collaboration is a priority for the National Association of School Psychologists, the American School Counselor Association, and the School Social Work Association of America. Empirical data confirming the link between service-learning and positive social, emotional, career, and academic outcomes are sufficient evidence that mental health professionals, together with classroom teachers, should strive to make service learning a vital part of the educative process.

Chapter 1 emphasizes the importance of service learning in fostering developmental assets in children and adolescents. Chapter 2 discusses positive and best practices in service learning that contribute to youth development. Chapter 3 considers implementation opportunities and challenges in scaling up service learning in schools. Chapter 4 reviews administrative issues in coordinating and conducting service-learning projects. Chapter 5 explores the process of change for individuals and systems. Chapter 6 highlights the implications of service learning for professional development.

1
Basics of Service Learning

There is considerable pressure to raise standards and reform schooling in the United States (e.g., No Child Left Behind [NCLB] Act of 2001). Few would argue that the goals of schooling are to raise both knowledgeable and socially responsible children. The challenge is how to motivate students to learn new information and to become socially responsible, that is, to care about others. School-based mental health professionals (school psychologists and school counselors) have long recognized the importance of social and emotional learning in schools. However, programs to enhance social and emotional learning are often introduced as disjointed initiatives that are not aligned with the mission for which schools are held primarily accountable, that is, academic achievement. After terrifying incidents of violence in schools such as Columbine and Paducah, social and emotional education cannot be ignored. There is an increasing concern among teachers, administrators, and the community at large about the need to thoughtfully address the socialization process of schooling.

A strategy to engage children and adolescents in building community while learning is gaining widespread acceptance across the United States—and beyond. According to the results of a national survey reported by Kielsmeier, Scales, Roehlkepartain, and Neal, (2004), 69% of K-12 public schools in the United States organize some form of community service that reaches an estimated 15 million students, and 30% of K-12 public schools arrange service learning, which connects service to the school curriculum, involving an estimated 4.5 million students. Service learning engages students in useful community activities that can be tied to social, emotional, career, and academic learning objectives. NCLB Act encourages service learning as a strategy to meet its goals.

Historical Overview

Although service learning has only recently become a buzzword, the concept can be traced to Dewey's ideal of experiential education that foreshadowed today's strategy of integrating community service with the school curriculum (Dewey, 1933, 1938). In the late 1960s, the Southern Regional Education Board (1970) coined the term "service learning" to refer to the integration of needed

3

tasks with educational growth. The passage of the National and Community Service Trust Act of 1993 boosted interest in service learning in the United States (Lankard, 1995) while the formation of the International Partnership for Service-Learning reflected growing worldwide interest (Berry & Chisholm, 1999). An annotated history of the development of service learning compiled by Titlebaum, Williamson, Daprano, Baer, and Brahler, (2004), is available through the Learn and Serve America's National Service-Learning Clearinghouse (www.servicelearning.org).

Consistent with Dewey's educational and social philosophies emphasizing experiential education and citizenship, the components of service learning—active participation, caring, community building—establish connections between school and the real world. The educational benefits of linking education with experience are well founded. Piaget (1972) introduced the notion that abstract thought develops on the basis of interactions with the environment. Cognitive theory and research support the idea that learning should be situated in a meaningful context (Brown, Collins, & Duguid, 1989; Resnick, 1987). Constructivists argue that students acquire knowledge from the social context in which they experience that knowledge (Rogoff, 1984).

Definition

Service learning is a form of experiential education where learning occurs through cycles of action and reflection as students work with others in applying their knowledge to solve a community problem and, at the same time, reflect upon their experience to gain a deeper understanding of complex issues for themselves. Reflection turns service into learning. Eyler and Giles (1999) cited three reasons why service learning contributes to students' understanding and ability to apply knowledge:

1. Deeper learning results because students are more engaged and curious about issues they experience in the community.
2. Students find that they can better remember material that they learn within community contexts.
3. Learning is rooted in personal relationships and in doing work that makes a difference in people's lives.

The most widely accepted definition of service learning is based upon the National and Community Service Act 1990, and includes the following four dimensions:

1. Students learn through participation in organized experiences that meet actual community needs and are coordinated with school and community.
2. The program is integrated into the academic curriculum with time to process those experiences.

3. Students are given opportunities to use their knowledge and skills in real-life situations in communities.
4. Learning is extended beyond the classroom into the community, which fosters the development of a sense of caring.

Service learning is a dynamic, reciprocal relationship between students and the community resulting in mutual benefits. Community can be broadly defined to include settings and situations within or outside of the school walls. Pritchard (2002) and Ammon (2002) noted considerable confusion about community service and service learning. Although the terms are often used interchangeably to refer to a relationship between the community and the school, the concepts and definitions of community service and service learning are quite different, which makes it difficult to interpret the statistics on current practices. Pritchard reviewed three data sets:

1. The 1999 US Department of Education study that examined the prevalence of community service and service learning in public schools across the country.
2. The Service-Learning Survey, which examined the prevalence in private schools.
3. The 1999 National Household Education Survey that examined prevalence in both types of schools.

The conclusion was that about three quarters of all schools participate in either community service or service learning; rates of participation were highest in secondary schools and lowest in elementary schools. However, in a survey of public school administrators who were given a definition of service learning that included clearly identified learning objectives and integration with the academic curriculum, only 32% reported that their schools were actually engaged in service learning.

Various service-learning programs assign different weight to the two components. Sigmon (1994) offers the following typology, suggesting four variations in the relationship between service and learning:

1. service LEARNING, where the emphasis is on learning objectives.
2. SERVICE learning that is service oriented.
3. service learning with separate service and learning goals.
4. SERVICE LEARNING, where service and learning goals are of equal weight and enrich each other.

SERVICE <=> LEARNING

Service learning can be either direct or indirect. In direct approaches, students engage in face-to-face interactions with people being served in the community. Common direct services include tutoring or assisting the elderly. Indirect approaches involve experiences that address a community need but in this case, the service providers and the recipients of service are physically distant from one another, such as in raising money for a family in need, in writing letters to people in the military, or in political advocacy for community needs. Indirect service-learning experiences also may take place at a service site, but may not involve direct contact with the recipients of service—entire communities rather than individuals benefit; for example, community beautification projects (Delve, Mintz, & Stewart, 1990; Dunlap, Drew, & Gibson, 1994).

The type and quality of the service-learning experience can affect its impact. Two aspects of K-12 service learning most closely associated with positive academic results are clear linkage with the curriculum and direct contact with those being served (Billig, 2003). In a pilot study conducted by Coomey and Wilczenski (2005), middle through high school students participating in direct service learning reported significantly greater social benefits than students participating in indirect service learning.

Service Learning as Social–Emotional Intervention

In addition to documenting the academic benefits of service learning, Billig's (2000, 2002, 2004) literature reviews revealed accumulating evidence of the social and emotional benefits as well. These benefits also extend to children and adolescents typically referred for mental health services; for example, students with disabilities and those at risk for behavioral and academic problems (Brigman & Molina, 1999; Duckenfield & Swanson, 1992; Kraft & Wheeler, 2003; Muscott, 2000; Piliavin, 2003; Shoultz, Miller, & Ness, 2001). For students with social and emotional problems, Kraft and Wheeler (2003) used service learning as a type of "group therapy" similar to cognitive behavior modification. In that context, service learning was expanded beyond academic goals to include affective and therapeutic components that stimulated the students' positive beliefs about themselves. Thus, there is a strong basis for employing service learning as a social–emotional intervention.

Although teachers, school administrators, and parents value social and emotional competence, they often express concern that focusing on social and emotional development will diminish academic achievement. Yet, considerable evidence indicates just the opposite effect—that social and emotional competence actually promotes resiliency and enables academic learning (Bear, Manning, & Izard, 2003; Buckley, Storino, & Saarni, 2003; Cohen, 1999, 2001; Elliott, DiPerna, Mroch, & Lang, 2004; Malecki & Elliott, 2002; Shapiro, 2000; Zins, Weissberg, Wang, & Walberg, 2004). For example, Caprara, Barbaranelli, Pastorelli, Bandura, & Zimbardo, (2000) found that prosocialness in childhood had a strong positive impact five years later on academic achievement and peer relationships in adolescence. Izard et al. (2001) also showed that emotional knowledge serves as a mediator of the effects of verbal ability on academic competence. That finding suggests that the ability to recognize emotional cues facilitates positive social interactions and that a deficit in this ability contributes to behavior and learning problems.

School psychologists and school counselors need to become more proactive than reactive in weaving social and emotional learning into the fabric of the school curriculum. Service learning is a strength-based intervention that can be a key strategy for coordinating academic and social–emotional learning initiatives. Elias et al. (1997) defined social and emotional learning as the process by which students learn to manage emotions, care about others, behave responsibly, and maintain positive interpersonal relationships. Furthermore, academic learning is only possible when students' social, emotional, and physical needs have been met (Collaborative for Academic, Social, and Emotional Learning [CASEL], 2003). Social and emotional skills are best developed in real-life situations with opportunities for practice and feedback (Cohen, 1999, 2001). Service learning provides authentic contexts for social and emotional learning (Fredericks, 2003).

Service Learning as Career Exploration

In addition to supporting academic skills, school psychologists and school counselors support the development of personal and social skills identified by the Secretary's Commission on Achieving Necessary Skills (SCANS, 1991) as needed by students for success in the workplace. The SCANS report encouraged schools to promote the employability skills, such as the personal qualities of responsibility, self-regulation, sociability, and integrity. The report urged educators to combine social–emotional and academic education. The School to Work Opportunities Act (US Department of Education, 1994) advocated collaborative programs that involved K-12 educators, business leaders, and higher education faculty in infusing career awareness, career preparation, and employability skills into the Kindergarten through 12th-grade curriculum.

Service learning offers students real-world, hands-on experiences to complement traditional classroom instruction. During the process of serving, students learn more about their strengths, interests, and a range of occupational possibilities. When students have a strong personal identity and understand the connection between their education and future career opportunities, they are more motivated to learn academic subjects (Sciarra, 2004). Service learning seamlessly integrates academic, career, and social–emotional education.

Ethical Foundations

Service-learning programs vary in their ethical foundations. Variations in the ethical grounding of service learning have moral and political implications for what students learn and what benefits accrue to the community (Donahue, 1999).

Battistoni (1997) identified two ethical foundations of service learning: philanthropic and civic. Kahne and Westheimer (1996) drew an important conceptual distinction between the two in describing service-learning goals of charity versus change. *Charity* is primarily a giving relationship that inculcates a sense of civic responsibility and fosters the development of altruism. The authors also pointed out that an emphasis on charity can support a conservative sociopolitical agenda by advancing volunteerism as an alternative to government programs. Conversely, *change* emphasizes the transformative potential of service learning.

Change involves a caring relationship that deepens understanding of others and the context of their lives. Emphasizing change through service learning carries the moral, political, and intellectual implications of caring and transformation. Students learn that social reform requires more than kindness.

Service-learning experiences are clearly oriented toward neither charity nor change. It is reflection that focuses the learning toward one direction or another. Consider the following questions: How did you feel after helping in the homeless shelter? Why are so many families in our community homeless? The first question orients the student toward charity and the answer is likely to raise self-esteem. The second question orients the student toward change and is likely to raise issues of poverty and social inequities. Transformation involves systematic and critical reflection with the hope that students' values and beliefs will be changed by their experiences. Students participating in service learning inevitably reflect upon issues of social justice they encounter in the community; perhaps fueling their concerns about injustice and energizing them to work for social change.

School psychology and counseling are essentially an ethic of care (Gilligan, 1982). School psychologists and school counselors have a special relationship with the community, that of caring for the educational and psychological well-being of its students. Service learning is one way for school psychologists and school counselors to apply that ethic of care in schools (Keller, Nelson, & Wick, 2003). Service learning can give students the opportunity to be involved in complex contexts and to grapple with situations that may challenge their fundamental assumptions about the world. Service learning should include opportunities for intentional reflection upon social justice issues and the welfare of those for whom they are caring.

Character Education

Service learning supports the ethical goals of character education (Lickona, Schaps, & Lewis, 2003; Schaffer, Berman, Pickeral, & Holman, 2001; Cohen, 2006) by providing situations where helping and collaboration, as well as sensitivity to culture and social justice issues, become integral parts of the educative process. There is a connection and synergy in combining service learning and character education. Service learning emphasizes the goals of character education by seamlessly weaving civility, ethics, and social responsibility into the school culture and curriculum (Berman, 2000; Character Education Partnership, 2001). Positive impacts have been reported concerning character development for students with emotional, behavioral, and learning disabilities and their nondisabled peers involved in an after-school service-learning program (Muscott, 2001; Muscott & O'Brien, 1999).

Character education and ethics are controversial issues in schools, with some individuals advocating a particular religious point of view and others advocating that schools take a neutral position on values. Berman (2000) suggested a middle path for schools in promoting collectively held values and character traits such as trustworthiness, respect, responsibility, justice, fairness, caring, and citizenship.

Swick et al. (2003, p. 8) described how those character traits relate to service-learning processes:

1-2 Character Traits	Service-Learning Processes
Moral language, open and fair communications, empathetic listening, responsible behavior	Students use all language arts skills (researching, writing, keeping journals, reflecting, sharing, presenting) and many math and science skills (predicting, charting, graphing, discovery, hypothesis testing, assessment, etc.) in designing and implementing their projects.
Moral problem-solving, ethical reasoning, fair decision-making	Students research real community needs, plan projects, design solution strategies, and solve problems in a fair and just manner to benefit the community.
Responsibility, integrity, self-control, punctuality, sensitivity, kindness, moderation, unselfishness	In carrying out their service-learning projects, students learn to act responsibly, control their behavior to benefit others, communicate with a variety of others of all ages. They must meet their obligations in a timely and courteous manner since others depend on them.
Equity and honesty	Students have to manage their own resources (time, space, materials, etc.) in concert with others. In order to get the job done they must share openly and honestly.
Caring, cooperating, resolving conflicts, helping others, trustworthiness, keeping promises, loyalty, empathy, and respect	Students must work and communicate together as a team. They must serve their clients who are often very different from themselves (age, ethnicity, economically, etc.) and they must rely on themselves to solve real-world problems.
Help others, act morally, practice good citizenship	Students deal with numerous external citizenship systems (schools, communities, agencies, and organizations) in which they must make ethical choices on an ongoing basis.
Responsible use, maintenance and care of equipment, materials, and supplies	Many service-learning projects use a variety of equipment, materials, and supplies which students must learn to use properly.

Service learning does not prescribe a specific character education program nor does it prescribe a particular set of values. The strength of service learning is its close connection with local community values. Through service learning, an ethic of care can be built into the culture of a school, which will give students new expectations about their behavior. By using service learning, school psychologists and counselors can reinforce the character traits that students will need to become caring, ethical adults.

Resilience

Everyone has heard the Horatio Alger rags-to-riches stories about how down-and-out youth can achieve the American dream of wealth and success through hard work, courage, and concern for others. Although many impoverished children do overcome tremendous odds to become successful, few do it alone. Resilient children usually have strong support network to assist them (Haggerty, Sherrod, Garmezy, & Rutter, 1996). Hillary Clinton (1996) reminded us of the African truism that it takes a village to raise a child. Schools *and* communities are needed to promote positive youth development.

Since the 1990s, there has been a paradigm shift in the field of psychology toward a positive development focus and strength-based approach. Instead of weaknesses, the search is for strengths and resilience despite exposure to stress. For Benard (2004), resiliency is the innate capacity for self-correction and survival in the face of adversity. Resilience derives from four basic strengths: social competence, problem solving, autonomy, and sense of purpose, which need to be nurtured through home, school, and community resources. School environments nourish resiliency by providing caring and supportive relationships, high expectations, opportunities for meaningful participation, and life skills development (Henderson & Milstein, 1996).

Dryfoos (1994) cited the following elements of successful resiliency building programs:

- Positive adult–youth relationships.
- Youth involvement in community and service opportunities.
- High expectations for students.
- Social–emotional and academic skills building.
- School and community collaboration to provide information and support services.
- Positive connecting strategies that involve adults, peers, recreation, and learning.

The elements identified by Dryfoos are common to quality service-learning programs. In service learning, the act of serving itself conveys a sense of caring. High expectations are communicated when students take on service projects to respond to a genuine community need. Students participate in meaningful ways when they assume ownership of both the service and the learning components of their projects. Through service learning, students experience real-world applications of a variety of skills for personal and interpersonal development as well as vocational exploration. Doll, Zucker, and Brehm (2004) discussed resilient classrooms as healthy learning environments. Service learning is a strategy to create those resilient classrooms.

Understanding Developmental Assets

Developmental assets is a philosophy for understanding a broad spectrum of what young people need in order to be successful in life. The Search Institute (2000), an independent nonprofit organization whose mission is to provide leadership and knowledge to promote healthy children and communities, has identified 40 developmental assets. The assets are grouped into two types: external assets refer to the support and opportunities that are provided by family, peers, schools, and communities; internal assets focus on the capacities, skills, and values that develop within young people.

SEARCH INSTITUTE'S 40 DEVELOPMENTAL ASSETS

Search Institute has identified the following building blocks of healthy development that help young people grow up healthy, caring, and responsible.

EXTERNAL ASSETS

Support

1. Family support – Family life provides high levels of love and support.

2. Positive family communication – Young person and her or his parent(s) communicate positively, and young person is willing to seek advice and counsel from parent(s).

3. Other adult relationships – Young person receives support from three or more nonparent adults.

4. Caring neighborhood – Young person experiences caring neighbors.

5. Caring school climate – School provides a caring, encouraging environment.

6. Parent involvement in schooling – Parent(s) are actively involved in helping young person succeed in school.

Empowerment

7. Community values youth – Young person perceives that adults in the community value youth.

8. Youth as resources – Young people are given useful roles in the community.

9. Service to others – Young person serves in the community one hour or more per week.

10. Safety – Young person feels safe at home, school, and in the neighborhood.

Boundaries and Expectations

11. Family boundaries – Family has clear rules and consequences and monitors the young person's whereabouts.

12. School boundaries – School provides clear rules and consequences.

13. Neighborhood boundaries – Neighbors take responsibility for monitoring young people's behavior.

14. Adult role models – Parent(s) and other adults model positive, responsible behavior.

15. Positive peer influence – Young person's best friends model responsible behavior.

16. High expectations – Both parent(s) and teachers encourage the young person to do well.

Constructive Use of Time

17. Creative activities – Young person spends three or more hours per week in lessons or practice in music, theater, or other arts.

18. Youth programs – Young person spends three or more hours per week in sports, clubs, or organizations at school and/or in the community.

19. Religious community – Young person spends one or more hours per week in activities in a religious institution.

20. Time at home – Young person is out with friends "with nothing special to do" two or fewer nights per week.

INTERNAL ASSETS

Commitment to Learning

21. Achievement motivation – Young person is motivated to do well in school.

22. School engagement – Young person is actively engaged in learning.

23. Homework – Young person reports doing at least one hour of homework every school day.

24. Bonding to school – Young person cares about her or his school.

25. Reading for pleasure – Young person reads for pleasure three or more hours per week.

Positive Values

26. Caring – Young person places high value on helping other people.

27. Equality and social justice – Young person places high value on promoting equality and reducing hunger and poverty.

28. Integrity – Young person acts on convictions and stands up for her or his beliefs.

29. Honesty – Young person "tells the truth even when it is not easy."

30. Responsibility – Young person accepts and takes personal responsibility.

31. Restraint – Young person believes it is important not to be sexually active or to use alcohol or other drugs.

Social Competencies

32. Planning and decision making – Young person knows how to plan ahead and make choices.

33. Interpersonal competence – Young person has empathy, sensitivity, and friendship skills.

34. Cultural competence – Young person has knowledge of and comfort with people of different cultural/racial/ethnic backgrounds.

35. Resistance skills – Young person can resist negative peer pressure and dangerous situations.

36. Peaceful conflict resolution – Young person seeks to resolve conflict nonviolently.

Positive Identity

37. Personal power – Young person feels he or she has control over "things that happen to me."

38. Self-esteem – Young person reports having a high self-esteem.

39. Sense of purpose – Young person reports that "my life has a purpose."

40. Positive view of personal future – Young person is optimistic about her or his personal future.

These developmental assets are experiences and personal qualities that people generally agree are desirable for youth. The Search Institute (2003) reported troubling results of a large-scale survey indicating that the average young person obtains only 18.6 of the 40 assets. Furthermore, young people's experience of most of these developmental assets declines over the middle school years (Scales,

2005). Society has simply not been successful in promoting positive youth development. Service learning, however, holds promise as a core strategy for building developmental assets and the developmental assets framework can be used to strengthen service-learning project designs. The Search Institute (2000) identified service-learning connections to the eight categories of developmental assets.

SERVICE-LEARNING CONNECTIONS TO THE EIGHT CATEGORIES OF DEVELOPMENTAL ASSETS

Asset Category	Description	Service-Learning Connections
1. Support	Young people need to experience care, love, and involvement from their family, neighbors, and many others. They need organizations and institutions that provide positive, supportive environments.	Working together on service-learning projects can cement relationships of support and caring between peers and with parents and other adults.
2. Empowerment	Young people need to be valued by their community and have opportunities to contribute to others. For this to occur, they must feel safe.	As they contribute to their world, young people become experts about issues that are important to them, and are seen and see themselves as valuable resources for their organizations and communities. Careful preparation and good supervision during their service-learning efforts help them feel safe.
3. Boundaries and expectations	Young people need to know what is expected of them and whether behaviors are "in bounds" or "out of bounds".	Boundaries and expectations are reinforced when activities include ground rules for involvement and as adults and peers become positive role models for each other.
4. Constructive use of time	Young people need constructive, enriching opportunities for growth through creative activities, youth programs, involvement with a center or worship or spirituality, and quality time at home.	Service-learning provides opportunities for young people to use their time to expand their minds and hearts, offer hope and support to others, and use their creativity to deal with new challenges and opportunities.
5. Commitment to learning	Young people need to develop a lifelong commitment to education and learning.	Education linked to action can unleash a new commitment to learning as youth apply their knowledge to issues and problems and as they are exposed to questions and situations that challenge their worldview and perspectives.
6. Positive values	Young people need to develop strong values that guide their choices.	Through service-learning, young people not only express their positive values, they also have opportunities to affirm and internalize values that are important to them.
7. Social competencies	Young people need skills and competencies that equip them to make positive choices, to build relationships, and to succeed in life.	Many skills and social competencies are nurtured as young people plan their activities, take action, and build relationships with their peers, adults who serve them, and service recipients.
8. Positive identity	Young people need a strong sense of their own purpose, power, and promise.	Service-learning becomes an important catalyst for shaping positive identity as young people discover their gifts and a place in the world through their acts of service and justice.

Service learning enriches the lives of all students by building developmental assets that foster resiliency as a protective factor to counterbalance risk factors due to a lack of bonding to family, school, and community. Service learning benefits students socially, emotionally, and academically (Eyler & Giles, 1999): Cognitive gains are reported, such as problem-solving ability in applying abstract concepts to real-life issues and in increasing motivation to learn. Studies of service learning have documented gains in students' self-esteem and sense of personal efficacy in making meaningful contributions to the community. Gains are also evident in students' ability to empathize with individuals experiencing social injustices. The Search Institute (2000, p. 14) summarized the following favorable service-learning outcomes that increase internal developmental assets:

Commitment to Learning

- Grades
- School attendance and performance
- Commitment to class work
- Working for good grades

Positive Values

- Prosocial and moral reasoning
- Empathy
- Personal and social responsibility
- Perceived duty to help others
- Altruism
- Concern for others' welfare
- Awareness of societal problems

Social Competencies

- Self-disclosure
- Development of mature relationships
- Social competence outside of school
- Problem-solving skills

Positive Identity

- Self-concept
- Self-esteem
- Self-efficacy

There are many good reasons for engaging students in asset-building service learning (Search Institute, 2000, p. 8):

For the Students

- Engaging in service can be a gateway asset enabling other assets.
- Service learning changes others' perceptions of students from problems to resources.
- Enhances learning and leadership through active, hands-on experiences.
- Connects students with caring and responsible adults and peers.

For Sponsoring Organizations

- Service learning may be a powerful strategy for fulfilling their organization's mission.
- It provides a service to those in need.
- It can energize an organization through the students' commitment and enthusiasm.

For the Recipients of Service

- Service learning meets real needs.
- It provides an opportunity to build relationships with young people.
- It can offer hope and confidence in the goodwill of others.

For the Larger Community

- Students bring new energy, capabilities, and ideas for addressing needs and building community.
- Service learning cultivates a new generation of caring citizens.
- Students are seen as valuable community resources.

Conceptually, the flow chart depicts the relationships between service learning, developmental asset building and social, emotional, career, and academic outcomes:

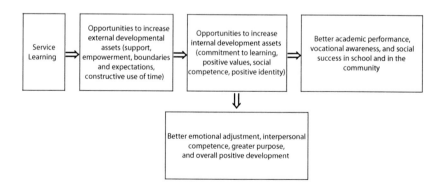

Goals of School Psychologists and School Counselors in Implementing Service Learning

Engaging students in authentic and meaningful learning contexts through service learning is a promising strategy for prevention and/or intervention. Service learning contributes to students' resiliency, dispositions, and resources in making alternative (to maladaptive) choices of behavior, and for those at risk for social and emotional problems (e.g., depression) in finding purpose in activities beyond themselves.

The goals of school psychologists and school counselors in implementing service learning are to:

- provide opportunities for student success, thus closing the achievement gap;
- increase equity in access to strength-based mental health interventions;
- support teachers in strategies to address learning and behavior problems in the classroom;
- develop essential social, emotional, career, and academic competencies for student success and post-secondary transition;
- assist career planning and decision making for all students;
- coordinate staff, parents/caregivers, and community resources
- analyze service-learning outcomes and variables for school improvement planning
- partner with business and industry to design programs that ensure students' workplace readiness

New Roles

The Center for Mental Health in Schools at UCLA (2001) is seeking to restructure mental health services in schools. The center envisions systemic collaboration among school psychologists, school counselors, and school social workers to ensure seamless prevention and intervention programming, not only for individual students but for classrooms and schools as well. A strength-based focus is recommended, emphasizing asset-building, protective factors and resilience to support positive youth development.

School-based mental health professionals cannot lose sight of their primary responsibility in helping *all* students achieve in school, and in particular, meeting the needs of traditionally underserved students (National Center for Transforming School Counseling, 2003). Hart and Jacobi (1992) lamented the fact that mental health professionals and teachers are poorly integrated in their work in schools. Too often social and emotional learning is the domain of school psychologists and counselors, not the whole school. Rather than taking exclusive responsibility for social and emotional learning, mental health professionals need to create a network of school and community resources to enhance positive student development. Service learning can be the vehicle for coordinated and systemic interventions among mental health professionals.

Service learning can also connect the work of mental health professionals with the work of teachers to fulfill the academic and citizenship goals of schools. For example, Stott and Jackson (2005) described the success of project ACCEPT (Alliance for Children: Collaborative Exceptional Peer Tutors), a service-learning class cotaught by school counselors and teachers to help middle school students reach personal, social, career, and academic learning goals. Brigman and Molina (1999) explained the *Living, Learning, Working Program*, a service-learning activity that enlisted fourth- and fifth-grade students to assist younger students. The older children were trained to read prosocial stories to younger children and to discuss social problem solving. The older children modeled listening, attending, empathy, social problem-solving, and helping skills for the younger students, and, in so doing, reinforced their competence in those key interpersonal skills.

Many school-based mental health professionals are overwhelmed with referrals for individual counseling. The profession needs to move beyond trying to solve problems one by one and deal with larger issues. Feelings of alienation and purposelessness expressed by young people are witnessed in the lack of youth engagement in schools and communities. Peterson and Seligman (2004) suggested that engagement might be a necessary condition for positive youth development. Service learning is a more efficient, alternative intervention that fosters student engagement and is likely to produce gains in personal, social, career, and academic learning.

References

Ammon, M.S. (2002). Probing and promoting teachers' thinking about service-learning: Toward a theory of teacher development. In S.H. Billig & A. Furco (Eds.), *Service-learning through a multi-disciplinary lens* (pp. 33–54). Greenwich, CT: Information Age Publishers.

Battistoni, R. (1997). Service-learning and democratic citizenship. *Theory into Practice, 36*, 150–156.

Bear, G.G., Manning, M.A., & Izard, C.E. (2003). Responsible behavior: The importance of social cognition and emotion. *School Psychology Quarterly, 18*, 140–157.

Benard, B. (2004). *Resiliency: What we have learned.* San Francisco, CA: West Ed.

Berman, S.H. (2000, March 1). *Building a nation of citizens—The role of character education in America's schools.* Testimony on Education and the Workforce House Subcommittee on Early Childhood, Youth, and Families. Retrieved November 26, 2003, from http://edworkforce.house.gov/hearings/106th/ecyf/charactered3100/berman.htm.

Berry, H.A., & Chisholm, L.A. (1999). *Service-learning in higher education around the world: An initial look.* (ERIC Document Reproduction Service No. ED 439 654).

Billig, S.H. (2000). Research on K-12 school-based service-learning: The evidence builds. *Phi Delta Kappan, 81*, 658–664.

Billig, S.H. (2002). Support for K-12 service-learning practice. A brief review of the research. *Educational Horizons, 80*, 184–189.

Billig, S.H. (2003). *Using evidence to make the case for service-learning as an academic achievement intervention in K-12 schools.* Retrieved August, 19, 2005, from http://www.seanetonline.org/images/UsingEvidencetoMaketheCaseforService.doc.

Billig, S.H. (2004). Heads, hearts, and hands: The research on K-12 service-learning. In *Growing to greatness: The state of service-learning project* (pp. 12–25). St. Paul, MN: National Youth Leadership Council.

Brigman, G., & Molina, B. (1999). Developing social interest and enhancing school success skills: A service-learning approach. *Journal of Individual Psychology, 55,* 342–354.

Brown, J.S., Collins, A., & Duguid, P. (1989). Situated cognition and the culture of learning. *Educational Researcher, 18*(1), 32–42.

Buckley, M., Storino, M., & Saarni, C. (2003). Promoting emotional competence in children and adolescents: Implications for school psychologists. *School Psychology Quarterly, 18,* 177–191.

Caprara, G.V., Barbaranelli, C., Pastorelli, C., Bandura, A., & Zimbardo, P.G. (2000). Prosocial foundations of children's academic achievement. *Psychological Science, 11,* 302–306.

Center for Mental Health in Schools. (2001, March). *Framing new directions for school counselors, psychologists, and social workers.* UCLA: Author. Retrieved August 25, 2005, from http://smhp.psych.ucla.edu/pdfdocs/Report/framingnewdir.pdf.

Character Education Partnership. (2001). *Service learning and character education: One plus one is more than two.* Washington, DC: Author.

Clinton, H.R. (1996). *It takes a village and other lessons children teach us.* New York: Simon & Schuster.

Cohen, J. (Ed.). (1999). *Educating minds and hearts: Social emotional learning and the passage into adolescence.* New York: Teachers College Press.

Cohen, J. (Ed.). (2001). *Caring classrooms/intelligent schools: The social emotional education of young children.* New York: Teachers College Press.

Cohen, J. (2006). Social, emotional, ethical, and academic education: Creating a climate for learning, participation in democracy, and well-being. *Harvard Educational Review, 76,* 201–237.

Collaborative for Academic, Social, and Emotional Learning [CASEL]. (2003). *Safe and sound: An educational leader's guide to evidence-based social and emotional learning programs.* Chicago, IL: University of Illinois.

Coomey, S.M., & Wilczenski, F.L. (2005, November). *Does the service matter? Comparative benefits of direct and indirect service-learning experiences.* Paper presented at the International Service-learning Research Conference, Michigan State University, East Lansing, MI.

Delve, C.I., Mintz, S.D., & Stewart, G.M. (1990). Promoting values development through community service: A design. In C.I. Delve, S.D. Mintz, & G.M. Stewart (Eds.), *Community service as values education: New directions for student services,* no. 50 (pp. 7–29). San Francisco: Jossey-Bass.

Dewey, J. (1933). *How we think.* Boston: Heath.

Dewey, J. (1938). *Experience and education.* New York: Collier.

Doll, B., Zucker, S., & Brehm, K. (2004). *Resilient classrooms: Creating healthy environments for learning.* New York: Guilford Press.

Donahue, D.M. (1999). Service-learning for preservice teachers: Ethical dilemmas for practice. *Teaching and Teacher Education, 15,* 685–695.

Dryfoos, J. (1994). *Full service schools: A revolution in health and human services for children, youth, and families*. San Francisco: Jossey-Bass.

Duckenfield, M., & Swanson, L. (1992). *Service-learning: Meeting the needs of youth at risk*. Clemson University: National Dropout Prevention Center.

Dunlap, N.C., Drew, S.F., & Gibson, K. (1994). *Serving to learn: High school manual*. Columbia, SC: South Carolina Department of Education.

Elias, M.J., Zins, J.E., Weissberg, R.P., Frey, K., Greenberg, M., Haynes, N., et al. (1997). *Promoting social and emotional learning: Guidelines for educators*. Alexandria, VA: Association for Supervision and Curriculum.

Elliott, S.N., DiPerna, J.C., Mroch, A.A., & Lang, S.C. (2004). Prevalence and patterns of academic enabling behaviors: An analysis of teachers' and students' ratings for a national sample of students. *School Psychology Review, 33*, 302–309.

Eyler, J., & Giles, D.E. (1999). *Where's the learning in service learning?* San Francisco, CA: Jossey-Bass.

Fredericks, L. (2003). *Making the case for social and emotional learning and service learning*. Denver, CO: Education Commission of the States.

Gilligan, C. (1982). *In a different voice: Psychological theory and women's development*. Cambridge, MA: Harvard University Press.

Haggerty, R.J., Sherrod, L.R., Garmezy, N., & Rutter, M. (Eds.). (1996). *Stress, risk, and resilience in children and adolescence: Processes, mechanisms, and interventions*. New York: Cambridge University Press.

Hart, P.J., & Jacobi, M. (1992). *From gatekeeper to advocate: Transforming the role of the school counselor*. New York: College Entrance Examination Board.

Henderson, N., & Milstein, M. (1996). *Resiliency in schools*. Thousand Oaks, CA: Corwin Press.

Izard, C., Fine, S., Schultz, D., Mostow, A., Ackerman, B., & Youngstrom, E. (2001). Emotion knowledge as a predictor of social behavior and academic competence in children at risk. *Psychological Science, 12*, 18–23.

Kahne, J., & Westheimer, J. (1996). In the service of what? The politics of service learning. *Phi Delta Kappan, 77*, 593–599.

Keller, J., Nelson, S., & Wick, R. (2003). Care ethics, service-learning, and social change. *Michigan Journal of Community Service-learning, 10*, 39–50.

Kielsmeier, J.C., Scales, P.C., Roehlkepartain, E.C., & Neal, M. (2004). Community service and service-learning is public schools. *Reclaiming Children and Youth, 13*, 138–143.

Kraft, N., & Wheeler, J. (2003). Service-learning and resilience in disaffected youth: A research study. In S.H. Billig & J. Eyler (Eds.), *Deconstructing service-learning: Research exploring context, participation, and impacts* (pp. 213–238). Greenwich, CT: Information Age Publishing.

Lankard, B.A. (1995). *Service-learning: Trends and issues*. (ERIC Document Reproduction Service No. ED 384 737).

Lickona, T., Schaps, E., & Lewis, C. (2003). *CEP's eleven principles of effective character education*. Washington, DC: Character Education Partnership. Retrieved June 5, 2006, from http://www.character.org.

Malecki, C.K., & Elliott, S.N. (2002). Children's social behaviors as predictors of academic achievement: A longitudinal analysis. *School Psychology Quarterly, 17*, 1–23.

Muscott, H.S. (2000). A review and analysis of service-learning programs involving students with behavioral disorders. *Education and Treatment of Children, 23*, 346–368.

Muscott, H.S. (2001, Summer). Service-learning and character education as "antidotes" for children with egos that cannot perform. *Reclaiming Children and Youth, 10*(2), 91–99.

Muscott, H.S., & O'Brien, S.T. (1999). Teaching character education to students with behavioral and learning disabilities through mentoring relationships. *Education and Treatment of Children, 22*, 373–390.

National Center for Transforming School Counseling. (2003). *Mission statement.* Washington, DC: Author.

National and Community Service Act. (1990). Pub. L. No. 101–610.

No Child Left Behind [NCLB] Act. (2001). Pub. L. No. 107–110.

Peterson, C., & Seligman, M.E.P. (2004). *Character strengths and virtues: A handbook and classification.* New York: Oxford University Press and Washington, DC: American Psychological Association.

Piaget, J. (1972). Intellectual evolution from adolescence to adulthood. *Human Development, 16*, 346–371.

Piliavin, J.A. (2003). Doing well by doing good: Benefits for the benefactor. In C.L.M. Keyes & J. Haidt (Eds.), *Flourishing: Positive psychology and the life well-lived* (pp. 227–247). Washington, DC: American Psychological Association.

Pritchard, I. (2002). Community service and service-learning in America: The state of the art. In A. Furco & S.H. Billig (Eds.), *Service-learning: The essence of the pedagogy* (pp. 3–21). Greenwich, CT: Information Age Publishers.

Resnick, L. (1987). The 1987 AERA Presidential Address: Learning in school and out. *Educational Researcher, 16*(9), 13–20.

Rogoff, B. (1984). Introduction: Thinking and learning in a social context. In B. Rogoff & J. Lave (Eds.), *Everyday cognition: Its development and social context* (pp. 1–8). Cambridge, MA: Harvard University Press.

Scales, P.C. (2005). Developmental assets and the middle school counselor. *Professional School Counseling, 9*, 104–111.

Schaffer, E., Berman, S., Pickeral, T., & Holman, E. (2001). *Service-learning and character education: One plus one is more than two.* Denver, CO: Education Commission of the States.

Sciarra, D.T. (2004). *School counseling: Foundations and contemporary issues.* Belmont, CA: Brooks-Cole.

Search Institute. (2000). *An asset builder's guide to service-learning.* Minneapolis, MN: Author.

Search Institute. (2003). *Levels of assets among young people.* Minneapolis, MN: Author. Retrieved June 21, 2006, from http://www.search-institute.org/research/assets/assetlevels.html.

Secretary's Commission on Achieving Necessary Skills. (1991). *What work requires of schools: A SCANS report for America 2000.* Washington, DC: US Department of Labor.

Shapiro, E.S. (2000). School psychology from an instructional perspective: Solving big, not little problems. *School Psychology Review, 29*, 560–572.

Shoultz, B., Miller, E.E., & Ness, J. (2001). Volunteerism by persons with developmental disabilities [Special Issue]. *Impact, 14*(2).

Sigmon, R.L. (1994). *Linking service with learning.* Washington, DC: Council of Independent Colleges. Available at http://www.cic.edu.

Southern Regional Education Board. (1970). *Atlanta service-learning conference report.* Atlanta, GA: Author.

Stott, K.A., & Jackson, A.P. (2005). Using Service-learning to achieve middle school comprehensive guidance program goals. *Professional School Counseling, 9,* 156–159.

Swick, K.J., Winecoff, L., Nesbit, B., Kemper, R., Rowls, M., Freeman, N.K., et al. (2003). *Service-learning and character education: Walking the talk.* South Carolina: Department of Education.

Titlebaum, P., Williamson, G., Daprano, C., Baer, J., & Brahler, J. (2004). *An annotated history of service-learning.* Dayton, OH: University of Dayton. Available at Learn and Serve America's National Service-Learning Clearinghouse. http://www.servicelearning.org.

US Department of Education. (1994). *School to work opportunities act.* Washington: DC: Author.

Zins, J.E., Weissberg, R.P., Wang, M.C., & Walberg, H.J. (Eds.). (2004). *Building academic success on social emotional learning.* New York: Teachers College Press.

2
Positive and Best Practices in Service Learning

Toward Positively Oriented Practice

As the 20th century ended, Seligman and Csikszentmihalyi (2000) called for the study of positive psychology to shift thinking among mental health professionals away from a pathology orientation. A positive psychology orientation contradicts the emphasis on deficit-seeking activities and remedial interventions prevalent in the mental health field. Instead, positive psychology focuses on a person's strengths to maximize his or her full potential. Peterson and Seligman (2004, p. 3) recently devised a system, in contrast to the American Psychiatric Association's Diagnostic and Statistical Manual of Mental Disorders (APA, 1994), for classifying positive character traits and virtues with the stated goal of constructing a "manual of the sanities." The authors' intention is to generate consensual classification and assessment approaches for positive traits that will ultimately lead to the development of effective interventions to prevent mental illness and to promote psychological health.

The application of a positive psychology approach goes beyond prevention initiatives, which are often oriented toward reducing risk behaviors and treating discrete problems, to promote wellness as a valuable end in itself (Adelman & Taylor, 2000). Several major professional organizations concerned with mental health services in schools echoed the call for positively oriented mental health programming and its integration in the schools (American School Counselor Association [ASCA], 2003; National Association of School Psychologists [NASP], 2000; School Social Work Association of America [SSWAA], 2003). Schools are one of the few community agencies that maintain continuous involvement with children and families over time and, therefore, are uniquely positioned to take a positive development stance (Terjesen, Jacofsky, Froh, & DiGiuseppe, 2004).

Larson (2000) pointed out that high rates of boredom, alienation, and disconnection from meaningful challenges and purpose in life among students are not signs of psychopathology in most cases, but rather signs of a deficiency

21

in positive development. When dealing with youth issues, Catalano, Berglund, Ryan, Lonczak, and Hawkins (2004) advocated for a change in focus from single behavior problem interventions to positive youth development programs. Their literature review indicated that programs addressing positive youth development constructs, such as social/emotional competency, resilience, and purpose, definitely made a difference in promoting positive behavior outcomes and in preventing behavior problems.

At the Search Institute (see http://www.search-institute.org), researchers are studying the attitudinal and behavioral risk and protective factors that are related to positive development among youth. Forty developmental assets, which refer to personal qualities and life experiences, have been identified as the building blocks of healthy development (Search Institute, 2006). Children and adolescents with fewer assets are at greater risk of negative developmental outcomes. Internal assets are concerned with identity (sense of purpose, self-esteem, personal power, positive view of the future) and with positive values (caring, social justice, integrity, honesty, responsibility, restraint) as well as social competence and commitment to learning. External assets refer to the positive experiences that children and adolescents receive from their environment. These assets are about supporting and empowering youth, about setting boundaries and expectations, and about positive and constructive use of time. External assets emphasize the role of families, schools, and the community.

Promoting Purpose in Youth

Damon (1995) specifically highlighted the importance of *purpose* for the positive development of youth. He cited research indicating that the emotional effects of purposelessness may include self-absorption, depression, psychosomatic complaints, as well as addiction, and that the social effects may include deviant and destructive behavior, lack of productivity, and an inability to maintain interpersonal relationships. On the positive side, purpose during youth leads to desirable outcomes, such as prosocial behavior, moral commitment, academic achievement, and high self-esteem. Damon, Menon, & Bronk (2003, p. 121) defined purpose as "a stable and generalized intention to accomplish something that is at once meaningful to the self and of consequence to world beyond the self." This definition highlights purpose as a personal search for meaning, but also emphasizes an external component, that is, the desire to make a difference in the world and contribute in ways that are larger than the self. As Damon and his coworkers pointed out, in the post-9/11 world, it is crucial to find ways to discourage purposes that lead to destructive, inhumane acts, and to encourage purposes that promote human welfare and social justice. Promoting purpose in youth involves helping them develop clear vocational goals, make commitments to personal interests and activities, and establish strong interpersonal relationships.

How can an institution or environment build competencies and develop climates that foster positive characteristics? Chapouleas and Bray (2004) recommended incorporating positively oriented practices in school psychology. The Search Institute (2006) stressed "asset building," that is, deliberately finding ways for youth to experience more assets in their lives to foster healthy development. Service learning is a vehicle for asset building and the framework of developmental assets can be used as a guide to strengthen service-learning efforts (Search Institute, 2000). Scales and Roehlkepartain (2004) suggested that service to others is a "gateway" asset that leads to many other assets, including success in school. Service learning can contribute to students' existential well-being, that is, their sense of purpose, meaning, and life direction (Piliavin, 2003). Because of the connection between service and learning with real-world needs, it may be particularly motivating for students who cannot see a purpose to school. As a strength-based, positive development approach, service learning is antidote to deficit models that place the blame for problems within the student. Service learning provides an authentic learning context for developing purposes that support emotional self-development as well as social development in achieving goals that positively touch the lives of others (O'Flanagan, 1997).

Speculation about counseling in schools for the 21st century indicates that it will incorporate advocacy to increase students' developmental assets (Galassi & Akos, 2004). Mental health services will be based on positive psychology and characterized by strong school–community partnerships, emphasizing ecological, proactive, and systemic practice in order to promote resiliency and build competencies for all children (Adelman & Taylor, 2001). Service learning can enable those new professional roles and functions.

Authentically Affirming Diversity

Another compelling reason to use service learning is that all students can participate. Service can be a powerful bonding mechanism to unite students to solve problems that affect the community, whether that community is within or outside the school. Through a service-learning project, students from diverse cultural and income groups are brought together to work for a common purpose. Working in diverse groups gives students authentic opportunities to learn how to communicate clearly, how to negotiate, how to reach a consensus, and how to value the opinions and beliefs of others; in other words, how to affirm diversity. The most consistent outcomes of service learning are a reduction of negative stereotypes and an increase in the tolerance for diversity (Eyler & Giles, 1999).

Each of us bears multiple identities constructed by nationality, race, class, gender, sexual orientation, religion, age, and so on. Multicultural education centers on learning about that diversity, examining power relationships and inequality, and responding in a positive manner to sociocultural differences in schools and communities (Olson & Wilczenski, 1995). Multicultural education and social justice concerns are inextricably linked through service learning.

Service learning is an experiential, reflection-oriented approach that emphasizes equality, reciprocity, and empowerment, and in so doing, promotes the strength of cultural diversity. Multiculturalism in service learning requires that students examine their own privileged as well as marginalized identities and the way in which those identities affect participation in communities. Multicultural service-learning experiences that focus on social justice issues expose students to the societal conditions that create inequalities and require them to reflect upon their social responsibilities as community members.

Often, service-learning projects that affect culturally diverse, low-income communities involve volunteers assigned to "help." Quinn, Gamble, and Denham (2001) cautioned that care must be taken in assigning students to work in low-income or minority communities so that poverty or race are not equated with social problems and do not stigmatize a community. In preparation for service-learning placements, students should explore their own preconceived notions about communities that may be different from their own and how those notions would affect their interactions in those community contexts.

Schools typically work with immigrant students to prepare them for assimilating in American society. Immigrant students are often under pressure to reject their cultural heritage. Only knowledge tested on standardized exams is valued. The knowledge possessed by people in diverse communities is usually discredited or ignored. Rather than simply helping immigrant groups to adjust to mainstream society, service learning can be used to gain valuable knowledge and skills from immigrant cultures (see Service-Learning Network, 2002).

How can schools legitimize the knowledge in minority communities while teaching the skills needed for life in our technological society? Hammond and Heredia (2002) provided an example of the *Mustard Green Festival* at an elementary school with a large population of Southeast Asian refugees. Mustard greens are important to Mien families because it is a crop that grows in adverse conditions. A school-community garden project involved Mien families growing mustard greens and then partnering with the school cafeteria staff to prepare an ethnic lunch for a festival day. Students at the school were included in various phases of the project—planting, harvesting, or preparing the meal. In class, the students studied about the importance of the crop for its survival and economic value in Southeast Asia. On the day of the festival, a group of Mien sixth-grade students gave garden tours to younger students, describing how mustard greens are cultivated. Dual roles as teachers and as tour guides challenged the usually quiet Mien students to speak publicly in English. Mien parents also learned teaching skills through the project. When their farming knowledge was seen as legitimate content for academic subjects, Mien children and families gained a new appreciation of their cultural heritage.

Title III of NCLB (2001) supports service learning to enhance programs for English language learners. Through high-quality service-learning activities, students develop a sense of caring and responsibility, and understand good citizenship while learning to speak, read, and write English.

There are commonalities between service learning and Native American concepts of community (Dawson, Hall, & LaPointe, 2006; Weah, Simmons, & Hall, 2000). Service to others is inherent in traditional tribal community and spiritual concepts. Many Native American youth live in communities with significant needs. Tribal schools can enlist students as resources to address that needfulness while providing an academic curriculum that is culturally relevant. Service learning in tribal communities relates education to each person's and each community's orientation to land, history, and traditional values.

Native Americans are working to retain their cultural heritage. Dawson described a culturally relevant service-learning project among the Sitka Tribe in Alaska. Students interviewed the community's elders to transform oral histories into written histories. They also helped the elders translate their indigenous language into English. These service-learning projects helped to inspire students to know more about their tribal history and customs. Because service learning has the potential to increase students' academic achievement and sense of community it is suggested as a strategy to meet the goals of Title VII pertaining to Indian, Native Hawaiian, and Alaska Native education.

International service-learning projects can be arranged to raise students' awareness about the different cultures of the world and critical global issues. For example, the *Global Response Network* (see: http://www.globalresponse.org/kids_teachers.php) is dedicated to fostering partnerships to protect the global environment. Its website issues alerts about threats to the global environment and offers concrete suggestions for planning and implementing service-learning projects. Students can be involved in service-learning projects regarding environmental issues, such as letter writing campaigns to save rainforests or adopting an endangered species to save them from extinction. The *Youth Service America* website (http://www.ysa.org) also lists ideas for global service projects such as worldwide disaster relief efforts. At some high schools, service-learning projects have taken students to other countries for various humanitarian causes. Another resource is the *Institute for Global Education and Service-Learning* (see: http://www.igesl.org), a nonprofit organization that creates service-learning programs in collaboration with schools around the world.

Optimal multicultural service-learning experiences are collaborative relationships. To foster those collaborative relationships, students must cross cultural, linguistic, and economic boundaries to reach shared goals. Multicultural service learning is a way to affirm diversity while still meeting academic standards, and multicultural/multilingual service learning holds great promise for English language learners (Allen, 2000; Grassi, 2006). The *National Service-Learning Clearinghouse* has compiled a list of publications for teaching about diversity using service learning: Search *diversity* at http://www.servicelearning.org. The *National Youth Leadership Council* also lists many service-learning project examples focusing on diversity issues (see http://www.nylc.org/rc_projectexample_detail.cfm). A free video, *Learning in Deed: The Power of Service-Learning for American Schools* (2002), produced by the National Commission on Service Learning and available from the National

Service-Learning Clearinghouse, which tells the story of a partnership between the Turner Middle School (an inner city school) and the Haverford School (a private academy) at Tinicum Wildlife Refuge in Pennsylvania, is an excellent illustration of the value of service learning in fostering respect for diversity.

Strengthening Home–School Relationships

School reform efforts coupled with federal legislation such as the Elementary and Secondary Education Act (2001) have made parental involvement in schooling a national priority. Research demonstrates that family involvement in schools has numerous benefits for students (Henderson & Mapp, 2002), including:

- higher grades and test scores;
- better school attendance;
- consistent homework completion;
- more positive attitudes and behavior; and
- higher graduation rates.

Research also shows that when parents are engaged in their child's schooling, the parent's develop:

- an improved sense of self-esteem;
- stronger social support networks; and
- a greater understanding about teaching and learning activities (Mapp, 2003).

Servicelearning has the potential to create opportunities to connect families with schools and to positively impact parental involvement (Neal & Kaye, 2006). Parents benefit by participating in service-learning programs because they interact with school personnel and contribute to their child's learning in unique ways while they themselves develop educational leadership and advocacy skills. Programs, such as service learning, that empower parents may be especially effective in strengthening home–school relationships among inner-city and minority families (Abdul-Adil & Farmer, 2006).

Neal and Kaye (2006) offered concrete strategies for involving and sustaining parental engagement in service learning. For example, schools may organize a task force to specifically plan parental involvement in service-learning programs. Parents can be recruited to assist with the logistics of carrying out service-learning projects. Parents may also recruit other parents to assist with service learning or teach other parents about the benefits of parent/child reflection activities. Students can be enlisted to think of additional ways to involve parents in service learning. In some cases, parents may be the recipients of service-learning activities (e.g., computer literacy). Parents may support service-learning programs in multiple ways; for example, helping to plan the activities, providing transportation, chaperoning community projects, networking with community agencies, assisting with reflection activities, helping to secure funding, and serving as mentors (Kaye, 2001; Kraft, 1998).

In the same ways that it engages students, service learning engages parents in their child's education in meaningful and authentic ways. Through service learning, a culture of parental involvement that will sustain parental engagement can develop, particularly at the middle and high school levels when many parents assume they are no longer needed.

Best Practices in Service Learning

The following essential components for best practices in service learning incorporate the Alliance for Service-Learning in Education Reform (ASLER, 1995) standards of quality for school- and community-based service learning:

Integrated Learning

- The project has clearly articulated social, emotional, and academic goals that arise from broader classroom or school goals.
- The service informs the social, emotional, and academic learning content, and the social, emotional, and learning content informs the service.
- Life skills learned in the community are integrated back into the classroom.

High-Quality Service

- The service responds to an actual community need that is recognized by the community.
- The service is age-appropriate and well organized.
- The service is designed to achieve significant benefits for students and the community.

Collaboration

- The service-learning project is a collaborative effort among as many partners as is feasible: students, parents, community-based organization staff, school administrators, teachers, and recipients of service.
- All partners benefit from the project and contribute to its planning.

Student Voice

Students actively participate in:
- choosing and planning the service project;
- planning and implementing the reflection sessions, evaluation, and celebration;
- taking on roles and tasks that are appropriate to their age.

Civic Responsibility

- The service project promotes students' responsibility to care for others and to contribute to the community.
- By participating in the service-learning project, students understand how they can impact their community.

Reflection

- Reflection establishes connections between students' service experiences and the academic curriculum.
- Reflection occurs before, during, and after the service-learning project.

Reflection: The hyphen between Service and Learning

John Dewey (1933, 1938) laid the foundation for service learning and reflection as it is practiced today. Dewey believed that education should be interactive and should incorporate real-world experiences. He also recognized that learning occurs by reflecting on experience—not simply by the experience itself. Learning only occurs when experiences are reviewed and questioned. Reflective thinking is the deliberate contemplation of one's thoughts and actions to gain a better understanding. For Dewey, the process of reflection raises doubt or puzzlement from which thinking originates. This uncertainty is followed by a search for information to resolve the doubt or solve the puzzle. Reflection connects thinking and action.

Eyler and Giles (1999) suggested that reflection is the hyphen between service and learning. Toole and Toole (1995, p. 100) defined reflection as "the use of creative and critical thinking skills to help prepare for, succeed in, and learn from the service experience, and to examine the larger picture and context in which the service occurs." The definition of service learning incorporates *reflection*: Service learning is integrated into the academic curriculum with time to *process those experiences* (National and Community Service Trust Act, 1990). Kolb (1984) outlined the process of reflection. The process begins with a description and sharing of the "what" of student experiences, followed by the "so what" and then the "now what." Answers to these questions are linked in cycles throughout the service-learning experience (Eyler, 2001).

In service learning, reflection is the intentional consideration of experience in light of specific learning objectives (Bringle & Hatcher, 1999; Hatcher & Bringle, 1997; Honnet & Poulsen, 1989). Many educators assume that students will self-reflect on their learning experiences, but this is not always the case. Moreover, when reflection does take place, too often it is just a summary of the experience. Hatcher and Bringle (p. 157) believe that effective reflection activities must:

- link experience to learning objectives,
- be guided,

- occur regularly,
- allow for feedback and assessment, and
- include the clarification of values.

The following reflective processes, outcomes, and best practices are summarized in fact sheets prepared by RMC Research Corporation, (2003a, 2003b):
Stages of Reflection

1. Preservice: Students examine their beliefs, attitudes, and other issues as they prepare to engage in a service-learning project.
2. During service: Students learn from peers, ask questions, obtain feedback, and solve problems.
3. Postservice: Students look back on their beliefs and attitudes to assess their own development. They also evaluate the project and their problem-solving efforts.

Five Steps of Reflection

1. Remember and think about the experience.
2. Relate the current experience to prior experiences.
3. Enact the experience by participating in service learning.
4. Extend thinking about the experience at higher levels.
5. Revisit the experience by looking at its value and what else can be learned from it.

Outcomes of Reflection

1. Academic: Students gain a deeper understanding of what they learn, apply learning to real-life situations, and develop problem-solving skills.
2. Civic Engagement: Students express an openness to new ideas and a tolerance for diverse points of view, and increase their commitment to social justice.
3. Personal: Students become aware of changes within themselves, develop community, and gain a sense of control in their lives.

The personal benefits of service-learning reflection are especially important for students with social and emotional problems. Curwin (1993) discussed the "healing power" of altruism and believes that service learning allows students to substitute caring for anger and feelings of worth for low self-esteem. The findings of a pilot study conducted by McCarty and Hazelkorn (2001) indicated that reflection is essential to impact social–emotional learning. Two groups of students with social and emotional problems participated in an environmentally oriented service-learning project. Although both groups showed similar academic gains, only the group engaging in systematic and focused reflection throughout their experience showed gains in self-esteem, locus of control, and empathy for the environment.

Reflection activities can be arranged to accommodate all types of learners. For reflection to be effective, however, it is important that the facilitator stimulate thought and discussion through questioning, posing dilemmas, supplying thought-provoking quotes, and so on. The following are several output modalities for reflection:

Outlets for Reflection

Oral	Written
Group discussions	Journals
Presentations	Brochures
Q & A sessions	Poetry
Interviews	Newsletters
Debates	Petitions
Teaching	Riddles
Singing	Essays
Visual	**Logical/Mathematical**
Photography	Predictions
Skits	Measure outcomes
Powerpoint	Experiments
Scrapbooks	Charts
Charades	Graphs
Puzzles	Maps
Murals	Surveys

Technology can facilitate these reflection activities and can also support the development of a service-learning program legacy by storing information from year to year so that students and staff can learn from previous experiences. Guidebooks are available to assist with the development of reflection prompts and activities (Eyler, 2001; Eyler, Giles & Schmiede, 1996; National Youth Leadership Council, 1993; Silcox, 1993; Toole & Toole, 1995). RMC Research Corporation (2003b) has produced a compendium of ideas for service-learning reflection for grades K-12 that is downloadable from www.servicelearning.org or www.rmcdenver.com.

Service learning and reflection can be enhanced through children's literature. School psychologists and counselors can use the power of children's literature to increase knowledge about other cultures, address personal and social adjustment, raise career awareness, and promote citizenship. There are several resource guides listing children's books and videos that deal with service learning (see New Hampshire Charitable Foundation, n.d.; Providence College, 1999; Weatherford, 2005). Rudman's (1995) volume explains how to use children's books to teach about important personal and social issues.

The developmental assets framework can also be used to guide reflection (Search Institute, 2000). Students can be encouraged to view their service through an "asset lens" (p. 108). For example:

- *Support*: Who supported you today? How did you support others?
- *Empowerment*: Did you feel valued while you performed your service?

- *Boundaries and Expectations*: Who were the best role models at the site?
- *Constructive Use of Time*: What did you do today that made you feel "creative?"
- *Commitment to Learning*: Did your service get you interested in learning more about the subject?
- *Positive Values*: Do you see evidence that equality and social justice were valued in the community?
- *Social Competencies*: Did anyone pressure you to do anything that you did not want to do? How did you handle it?
- *Positive Identity*: Did your service experience introduce you to any new career interests?

Reflection in service learning incorporates critical and creative thinking by the students to assess what they learned, to consider how they were affected personally, and to understand and evaluate the impact of their work in the community. Bringle and Hatcher (1999, p. 180) explained, "Experience becomes educative when critical reflective thought creates new meaning and leads to growth and the ability to take informed action."

References

Abdul-Adil, J.K., & Farmer, A.D. (2006). Inner-city African American parental involvement in elementary schools: Getting beyond urban legends of apathy. *School Psychology Quarterly, 21*, 1–12.

Adelman, H.S., & Taylor, L. (2000). Moving prevention from the fringes into the fabric of school improvement. *Journal of Educational and Psychological Consultation, 11*, 7–36.

Adelman, H.S., & Taylor, L. (2001). *Framing new directions for school counselors, psychologists, and social workers*. Los Angeles, CA: Center for Mental Health in Schools. Retrieved May 9, 2006, from http://smhp.psych.ucla.edu/pdfdocs/Report/framingnewdir.pdf.

Allen, L. (2000, March). Involving English language learners in community-connected learning. *Perspectives on Policy and Practice*. Providence, RI: Northeast and Islands Regional Educational Laboratory at Brown University.

Alliance for Service-Learning in Educational Reform [ASLER]. (March, 1995). *Standards of quality for school-based and community-based service-learning*. Alexandria, VA: Author. Retrieved June 21, 2006, from http://www.servicelearning.org/filemanager/download/12/asler95.pdf.

American Psychiatric Association. (1994). *Diagnostic and statistical manual of mental disorders* (4th ed.). Washington, DC: Author.

American School Counselor Association [ASCA]. (2003). *The ASCA national model: A framework for school counseling programs*. Alexandria, VA: Author.

Bringle, R.G., & Hatcher, J.A. (1999, Summer). Reflection in service-learning: Making meaning of experience. *Educational Horizons, 77*, 179–185.

Catalano, R.F., Berglund, M.L., Ryan, J.A.M., Lonczak, H.S., & Hawkins, J.D. (2004). Positive youth development in the United States: Research findings on evaluations of positive youth development programs. *Annals of the American Academy of Political and Social Science, 591*, 98–124.

Chapouleas, S.M., & Bray, M.A. (2004). Introducing positive psychology: Finding a place within school psychology. *Psychology in the Schools, 41,* 1–5.

Curwin, R.L. (1993). The healing power of altruism. *Educational Leadership, 51*(3), 36–40.

Damon, W. (1995). *Greater expectations: Overcoming the culture of indulgence in our homes and schools.* New York: Free Press.

Damon, W., Menon, J., & Bronk, K.C. (2003). The development of purpose during adolescence. *Applied Developmental Science, 7,* 119–128.

Dawson, C.T., Hall, M., & LaPointe, L. (2006). Native American service-learning. In *Growing to Greatness: The state of service-learning project* (pp. 59–66). St. Paul, MN: National Youth Leadership Council.

Dewey, J. (1933). *How we think.* Boston: Heath.

Dewey, J. (1938). *Experience and education.* New York: Collier.

Elementary and Secondary Education Act. (2001). U.S.C. 107–110.

Eyler, J. (2001). Creating your reflection map. In M. Canada (Ed.), *Service learning: Practical advice and models* (pp. 36–43). San Francisco: Jossey-Bass.

Eyler, J., & Giles, D.E. (1999). *Where's the learning in service learning?* San Francisco: Jossey-Bass.

Eyler, J. Giles, D.E., & Schmiede, A. (1996). *A professional's guide to reflection in service-learning: Student voices and reflections.* Nashville, TN: Vanderbilt University.

Galassi, J.P., & Akos, P. (2004). Developmental advocacy: Twenty-first century school counseling. *Journal of Counseling and Development, 82,* 146–157.

Grassi, E. (2006, April). *Multilingual/multicultural service-learning: An innovative approach to instruction for second language learners.* Paper presented at the annual meeting of the American Educational Research Association, San Francisco, CA.

Hammond, L., & Heredia, S. (2002). *Fostering diversity through community service-learning.* Los Angeles, CA: Constitutional Rights Foundation. Retrieved March 8, 2006, from: http://www.crf-usa.org/network/net9_1.htm.

Hatcher, J.A., & Bringle, R.G. (1997). Reflection: Bridging the gap between service and learning. *College Teaching, 45,* 153–158.

Henderson, A.T., & Mapp, K.L. (2002). *A new wave of evidence: The impact of school, family, and community connections on student achievement.* Austin, TX: Southwest Educational Development Laboratory. Retrieved April 18, 2006, from http://www.directionservice.org/cadre/parent_family_involv.cfm.

Honnet, E.P., & Poulsen, S. (1989). *Principles of good practice in combining service and learning.* Wingspread Special Report. Racine, WI: The Johnson Foundation.

Kaye, C.B. (2001). *Parent involvement in service-learning.* Columbia, SC: Department of Education.

Kolb, D.A. (1984). *Experiential learning: Experience as the source of learning and development.* Englewood Cliffs, NJ: Prentice-Hall.

Kraft, N.P. (1998). Building collaborations to support service-learning. In S.H. Billig (Ed.), *Building support for service-learning* (pp. 67–88). Denver, CO: RMC Research Corporation.

Larson, R.W. (2000). Toward a psychology of positive youth development. *American Psychologist, 55,* 170–183.

Mapp, K.L. (2003). Having their say: Parents describe why and how they are engaged in their children's learning. *The School-Community Journal, 13,* 35–64.

McCarty, B., & Hazelkorn, M. (2001, Spring). Reflection: The key to social–emotional change using service-learning. *Beyond Behavior, 10*(3), 30–35.

National and Community Service Act. (1990). Pub. L. No. 101–610.

National Association of School Psychologists [NASP]. (2000). *Guidelines for the provision of school psychological services*. Bethesda, MD: Author.

National Youth Leadership Council. (1993). *Learning by giving: K-8 service-learning curriculum guide*. St. Paul, MN: Author.

Neal, M., & Kaye, C. (2006). Service-learning: A context for parent and family involvement. *Growing to greatness: The state of service-learning project* (pp. 53–58). St. Paul, MN: National Youth Leadership Council.

New Hampshire Charitable Foundation. (n.d.). *Books for children on philanthropy, volunteerism, and related themes*. Concord, NH: Author. Available at http://www.givingnh.org/care/2b1.html

O'Flanagan, B. (1997, Winter) Building purpose through service. *Reclaiming children and youth, 5(4)*, pp. 223–225, 228.

Olson, S., & Wilczenski, F.L. (1995). Multicultural issues and education relevant to school psychology practice. *School Psychology International Journal, 16*, 323–334.

Peterson, C., & Seligman, M.E.P. (2004). *Character strengths and virtues: A handbook and classification*. Washington, DC: American Psychological Association and New York: Oxford Press.

Piliavin, J.A. (2003). Doing well by doing good: Benefits for the benefactor. In C.L. Keyes & J. Haidt (Eds.), *Flourishing: Positive psychology and the life well-lived* (pp. 227–247). Washington, DC: American Psychological Association.

Providence College, Department of Education. (1999). *Service-learning and children's literature: A resource guide*. Providence, RI: Author. Available at http://www.servicelearning.org.

Quinn, S.C., Gamble, D., & Denham, A. (2001). Ethics and community-based education: Balancing respect for the community with professional preparation. *Family Community Health, 23*(4), 9–23.

RMC Research Corporation. (2003a). *Connecting thinking and action: Ideas for service-learning reflection*. Denver, CO: Author.

RMC Research Corporation. (March, 2003b). *Reflection: K-12 service-learning*. Denver, CO: Author. Retrieved June 5, 2006, from http://www.servicelearning.org/resources/fact_sheets/k-12_facts/reflection/.

Rudman, M.K. (1995). *Children's literature: An issues approach*, 3rd ed. New York: Longman.

Scales, P.C., & Roehlkepartain, E.C. (2004). Service to others: A 'gateway' asset for school success and healthy development. In *Growing to greatness: The state of service-learning project* (pp. 26–32). St. Paul, MN: National Youth Leadership Council.

School Social Work Association of America [SSWAA]. (2003). *SSWAA organizational mission statement*. Northlake, IL: Author.

Search Institute. (2000). *An asset builder's guide to service-learning*. Minneapolis, MN: Author.

Search Institute. (2006). *Developmental assets*. Minneapolis, MN: Author. Retrieved May 15, 2006, from http://www.search-institute.org.

Seligman, M.E.P., & Csikszentmihalyi, M. (2000). Positive psychology: An introduction [Special issue]. *American Psychologist, 55*(1).

Service-Learning Network. (Spring, 2002). *Fostering diversity through service-learning*. Los Angeles, CA: Constitutional Rights Foundation. Retrieved March 8, 2006, from http://www.crf-usa.org/network/net9_1.htm.

Silcox, H. (1993). *A how to guide to reflection: Adding cognitive learning to community service-learning programs*. Holland, PA: Brighton Press.

Terjesen, M.D., Jacofsky, J.F., Froh, J., & DiGiuseppe, R. (2004). Integrating positive psychology into schools: Implications for practice. *Psychology in the Schools, 41*, 163–172.

Toole, J., & Toole, P. (1995). Reflection as a tool for turning service experiences into learning experiences. In C. Kinsley & K. McPherson (Eds.), *Enriching the curriculum through service-learning* (pp. 99–114). Alexandria, VA: Association for Curriculum Supervision and Development.

Weah, W., Simmons, V.C., & Hall, M. (2000). Service-learning and multicultural/multiethnic perspectives. *Phi Delta Kappan, 81*, 673–675.

Weatherford, C.G. (2005). *Tales that teach: Children's literature and service-learning*. South Carolina: Department of Education.

3
Implementation Opportunities and Challenges

Scaling up Service Learning

Many service activities in schools start as goodwill gestures on the part of the school, e.g., charitable fundraisers. This type of activity is community service but not service learning. As these community service programs evolve, the educational value of service becomes increasingly apparent. Typically, there is a developmental progression from community service to service learning. When service and learning can be combined in the same activity, new opportunities emerge for students, schools, and communities.

In addition to setting goals, planning projects, and other implementation issues, school psychologists and counselors will gradually construct their own understanding of what they are trying to accomplish via service learning. Implementing quality service learning is more than doing a project, it also involves how mental health professionals think about and contextualize what they are doing in schools.

School psychologists and counselors can initiate service learning through their own counseling work with students in schools. They can also connect with ongoing service-learning projects initiated by teachers and establish learning goals for specific students referred for counseling. Service learning is a natural opportunity to promote personal, social, and career learning goals, which are inseparably tied to academic goals. Moving beyond the initiatives of individual school psychologists, counselors, or teachers, however, will require administrative support. The critical point in institutionalizing service learning is its link to the academic, career, and social–emotional learning goals of the entire school and school district.

Building Capacity

Impetus for service learning often comes from a small group of committed individuals. School psychologists and school counselors can provide the leadership to develop a service-learning program by highlighting the benefits that include (a) an authentic context for social, emotional, career, and academic learning; (b) a multifaceted experience that can accommodate students with different learning needs; and (c) an opportunity to meet needs for belonging, self-efficacy, and self-esteem.

Start by working with like-minded individuals, rather than trying to convert the skeptics. Identify other school psychologists and school counselors who recognize the importance of service for positive youth development and establish a service-learning resource team as a base of support and a forum to generate enthusiasm and ideas. Begin with small projects that take place within the schools, on school grounds, or nearby. Simple projects are easier to manage while the "bugs" are worked out. Although after-school and extracurricular programs have value, there is a better chance that service will be connected with various learning goals if the activities occur during the school day. For example, a reading buddies program can be arranged during the school day where older students with social or emotional difficulties read to kindergarten children during the time of their regularly scheduled group counseling session. If possible, involve students in the selection of the service experiences. Students learn more when they perceive that what they do has real meaning and when they can see the effect of their work. Keep in mind that the longer the time devoted to the service and reflecting upon the service, the greater the likelihood of learning in affective and academic areas (Shumer, 1997).

Deepening Practice

When introducing service learning to mental health professionals (and teachers), a shift in mindset has to occur. They need to understand that service learning is not an addition to their workload; rather, it is another way to do their work. They need to see that it enhances student learning as well as their own professional practices. It is important for them to understand that all students, regardless of ability levels, socioeconomic status, or number of discipline referrals, can gain valuable experience by participating in service learning and can change school culture for the better.

Service learning can create a more caring and respectful school community. Kielsmeier, Scales, Roehlkepartain, and Neal (2004) reported that the vast majority of principals responding to a national survey indicated that service learning positively impacted their students' academic achievement, with the strongest impacts being on students' citizenship and social–emotional development. Sustainable service-learning programs will need the support of school principals. There are a few simple ways to encourage that administrative support (Middle, 1998):

- Invite the administrators to participate in service-learning project.
- Have students write thank you notes to administrators for their encouragement and support of service learning.

- Involve the principal in media coverage.
- Encourage parents to contact school administrators about service learning.
- Inform the PTA/O and school committee about service-learning projects.
- Advertise service-learning projects in school newsletters.
- Keep administrators aware of projects and successes.
- Try to locate outside sources of funding for projects.

Institutionalizing Change

Berman (2000) described service as systemic reform and service learning as more than a series of one-time activities to teach children about helping others. The first step toward institutionalizing service learning is to incorporate it in the curriculum (Pritchard & Whitehead, 2004). Service learning needs to be a fundamental and cohesive strategy for the development of social, emotional, career, and academic skills that begins in preschool and extends through high school graduation. Administrative structures need to be in place in order to sustain service learning throughout each level in schools.

Elias, Zins, Graczyk, and Weissberg (2003) suggested several factors associated with successful and enduring program implementation:

- A committee to oversee implementation and to resolve problems.
- Involvement of like-minded individuals with a sense of program ownership.
- Ongoing opportunities for professional development, both formal and informal.
- Inclusion of all student populations.
- High visibility in the school and community.
- Linkage to the mission of the school and/or school district.
- Consistent support from school principals.

Steps for Implementation

The following implementation framework incorporates the steps for implementation and the essential elements for effective service-learning programs listed by Duckenfield and Swanson (1992) and by Institute for Global Education and Service-Learning (2003a):

1. *Preparation*: The first step consists of all the activities that take place prior to the service itself. Students need to know what is expected of them and what they can expect from the service project. This includes helping the students develop the knowledge and skills they need to accomplish the project. Clear learning outcomes should be established that require the students to be involved in the construction of their own knowledge. Students should be given ownership and an active role in the selection, design, implementation, and evaluation of the service-learning project. Preparation components include:

- identifying and analyzing the problem,
- selecting and planning the project, and
- training and orientation.

2. *Action*: This step is the service itself. Service can take many forms but the project should be developmentally appropriate for those performing the service. The project should meet a genuine need that is recognized as significant by both the students and the community at large. The service project should be connected to personal, social, career, and academic learning goals. Specific criteria include:

- meaningfulness,
- curricular integrity,
- adequate supervision,
- student ownership, and
- developmental appropriateness.

3. *Reflection*: It is important that students be given opportunities to process the service experience to make the connection to learning objectives. Reflection should occur before, during, and after the service. Service reflection is an ideal time to raise awareness of the value of diversity in terms of abilities, racial, religious, and cultural differences. Reflection can also promote communication and interaction within the school and with the outside community. Students can reflect through activities such as:

- discussions,
- journals,
- art.

4. *Evaluation and Revision*: Assessment should be ongoing to ensure objectives and standards are being met. It is important for ethically responsible practice to determine the impact of the service project on everyone involved, including students, school, and the community. At this point, the project may be reconfigured based on evaluative feedback. Assessments should be:

- formative and
- summative.

5. *Celebration*: Students and community members need to be recognized for the success of the service-learning project. Acknowledging achievements also provides closure to the service-learning experience. There are many ways to implement this final step:

- assemblies,
- certificates,

- media coverage,
- school web page,
- parties, and so on.

The Institute for Global Education and Service-Learning's (2003b) checklist for high quality service learning is a useful guide in designing programs:

High Quality Service-Learning Checklist

Service-Learning Component	Important Questions to Ask	Evidence from Project
PREPARATION/ PLANNING	Were there specific learning activities, training, orientation, or needs assessment done before the project? Was a time line created?	
MEANINGFUL SERVICE	Was a service provided to someone else? Was the service academically and developmentally appropriate?	
REFLECTION	Were there opportunities for participants to review, evaluate, or analyze their feelings and learning from the project?	
YOUTH VOICE & OWNERSHIP	Were the participants given opportunities to have a voice in selecting, designing, or implementing the project?	
GENUINE NEED	Did the project meet a real, recognized need in the community?	
CONNECTION TO LEARNING	Is there a clear connection to real skills, knowledge, or content learned by the participants?	
DIVERSITY	Did the project recognize diversity through its participants, practice and outcomes?	
PARTNERSHIPS	Was there interaction and collaboration with others in the community?	
ASSESSMENT	Was student mastery of learning and service goals measured?	
EVALUATION	Were participants involved in evaluating the project? Were project goals achieved? Community impacted?	

Reprinted with permission of the Institute for Global Education and Service-Learning, Levittown, PA.

Implementation Challenges

Students with disabilities or those at risk of school failure may present extra implementation challenges because of their needs for structure, limited social skills, cognitive impairments, or lack of motivation. However, service learning is a strength-based, practical approach that can engage disenfranchised students, promote a sense of self-worth, and alter pessimistic views about their ability to contribute to the community. Through service, students from diverse backgrounds or those with special learning needs are able to practice appropriate communication and social interaction in natural settings.

Muscott (2001) offered advice about addressing the unique challenges presented by individual students with special needs:

- Arrange projects that are of high interest to the students. Students interested in particular activities, e.g., art, music, photography, carpentry, will engage more readily in projects that include their interest areas.
- Allow students to choose among several projects.
- Match student talents to specific aspects of the project; for example, more verbal students might take a speaking role, those who like to work with their hands might take on a construction task, students with high energy may be assigned to tasks that require mobility.

Most service-learning programs are cooperative group projects that provide an ideal situation for interpersonal interaction and learning social skills. However, service-learning projects for special education classes need to be selected with the group's level of functioning in mind. Rockwell (2001) delineated the characteristics and needs of students at three stages of group development. Rockwell described Stage 1 as one with little or no group cohesion. She suggested projects where students can make a personal contribution to a group effort without having to interact with peers; for example, writing cards to members of the military or nursing home residents. During Stage 2, a sense of group identity begins to emerge and it is important that students be given opportunities to practice making decisions and cooperating with a peer, for example, working together to feed or groom animals in the classroom or at a shelter. At Stage 3, students are invested in their group and have mastered social skills in collaborating with others. They are ready to participate in larger group activities, perhaps a general education service-learning project.

Through their professional training in counseling, school psychologists and school counselors develop expertise in human interaction and reflection that can be invaluable resources in implementing service-learning projects. They can help guide reflection and help students integrate new experiences into their expanding value systems. They can help students connect service with vocational exploration. They can assist in designing cooperative group processes and in setting social and emotional goals.

Response to Intervention

Response to Intervention (RtI) is the practice of providing interventions matched to student needs (Batsche et al., 2005). RtI encompasses both general and special education and uses a multi-tier system of educational supports. Each tier includes an increasing intensity of supports to address the student's need. Supports are framed in terms of a hierarchy based on the nature and the comprehensiveness of the intervention as well as the degree of responsiveness or resistance of a student to a given type of intervention. Formative and summative evaluations are conducted to closely monitor student progress. Service-learning activities can be designed at all levels of intervention intensity. Batsche et al. described the following three-tier model of school supports:

Tier 1, *core instructional interventions*

- All students
- Preventive, proactive

Tier 2, *targeted group interventions*

- Some students (at risk)
- Approximately 15% of student population

Tier 3, *intensive interventions*

- Individual students
- Approximately 5% of student population

The goal of school-based interventions is to increase desirable behavior and to decrease undesirable behavior. However, interventions are usually directed at eliminating undesirable behavior rather than facilitating desirable behavior. Service learning is a strategy that fosters positive growth and increases developmental assets (Search Institute, 2000). Following the three-tier model, service-learning interventions can be applied at more intense levels if a student still requires social and emotional support after the application of less intense interventions.

In Tier 1, schools provide the curriculum, instruction, and organization that address the needs of the majority of students. Tier 1 also provides supports for teachers to deliver the program. School psychologists and counselors might conduct a needs assessment and then, for example, if classroom appearance is determined to be a problem because of litter and inappropriate trash disposal, a service-learning recycling project could be arranged to involve all the students. Teachers would use the service-learning project as an instructional strategy to meet their academic curriculum goals. Mental health professionals could incorporate social, emotional, and/or career learning goals. For example, the service project would meet social and emotional learning goals in teaching the students about community, collaboration, and contributing to the common welfare.

In Tier 2, the recycling project might be adapted for students who display a poor response to the classroom-wide school service-learning project in Tier 1. Perhaps a few students have difficulty collaborating and settling conflicts. Those students could work on the same recycling project but in more structured ways, perhaps with assistance from school psychologists or counselors. Social–emotional learning goals would be written to give students opportunities and strategies to manage conflict in carrying out the recycling service project. Service learning would provide an authentic context to teach conflict resolution skills.

In Tier 3, the intensity of intervention is increased and directed toward accelerating an individual student's rate of progress. Intervention may be supported by special education. A recycling project is multifaceted, making it easy to accommodate a student's special needs. Participation in service learning would be written into the student's Individual Education Plan (IEP), with specific social, emotional, career, and/or academic goals and objectives to be addressed through the recycling project. An inclusive service-learning project provides opportunities for students with disabilities to participate in general education activities.

School psychologists and counselors can conceptualize the severity of social and emotional problems from the perspective of RtI (Gresham, 1991, 2002, 2004). RtI takes an intervention rather than as assessment perspective (McNamara & Hollinger, 2003). Assessment resources can then be devoted to documenting the effectiveness of interventions. In this way, assistance to the student comes first and intervention results are used as part of the evaluation process. Data derived from students' responses to interventions, such as a service-learning experience, can assist in determining the need for further, more intensive interventions.

Evaluation

"In the No Child Left Behind Act, Congress refers to evidence-based or research-based education at least 130 times. Every program and initiative bears this requirement, presumably as an antidote to 30 years of considerable federal government investment in improving education that critics contend has yielded a succession of fads rather than proven success" (Lewis, 2003, p. 339). The No Child Left Behind (NCLB) Act of 2001 raised the bar for students to meet rigorous academic standards and to demonstrate "Adequate Yearly Progress." Certainly academic achievement is central to a quality education. However, educators agree that there are other equally important outcomes of schooling. Graduates should be:

- productive citizens and good family members,
- engaged in their communities,
- be able to get along with others,
- caring toward others.

These personal and social variables that enhance academic learning also need to be measured because they matter for success in school and in life (Duckenfield & Drew, 2006). In addition to academic achievement, measurable outcomes are essential to demonstrate the link between service learning and personal, social, and career development. Why evaluate? In this era of accountability, school psychologists and counselors need to ensure that their interventions are having the intended outcomes; in fact, they have an ethical responsibility to do so.

The most important question for school psychologists and counselors is: "How are students different because of our work?" To determine if a service-learning project is successful, both student and community outcomes will need to be evaluated. From the outset, evaluation should be built into the service-learning intervention design focusing on a key outcome: What information will indicate whether the program was successful? How are students and communities different because of the service-learning project? Evaluation should easily proceed from the project's learning goals and the service experience. Data should only be collected if it can be used to improve programs.

A participatory action research approach, which considers the context of schooling, is recommended to evaluate outcomes and improve practices both in schools and in communities (Cruz & Giles, 2000; Elias et al., 2003; Smink & Duckenfield, 1998). School psychologists and counselors are in the best position to witness the effects of their interventions on students and the community. Action research grows out of reflection and is a vehicle for professional and program development. In its simplest form, action research seeks to understand social systems and then to alter problems generated by those social systems. Using action research strategies, school psychologists and counselors study their own work and use the results to make improvements. Multifaceted interventions such as service learning also require efforts to determine the "active ingredients" or components of the intervention that are responsible for the observed changes in social, emotional, career, and academic learning (Billig & Eyler, 2002). Both quantitative and qualitative approaches can be employed to address service-learning processes as well as outcomes. Bradley (1996) suggested the following questions and strategies for answering questions about the effectiveness of service-learning interventions at both formative (process) and summative (outcome) stages of evaluation.

Formative Evaluation	
Questions	**Answers**
Is the service-learning project being carried out as planned?	Observations of program operations
	Interviews with all participants
Is the program operating efficiently?	Questionnaires for stakeholders
	Minutes of meetings

Summative Evaluation	
Questions	**Answers**
Did the program meet its goals and objectives?	Checklists of goals and objectives
What impact did service learning have on students skills, behavior, attitudes, and developmental assets?	Surveys and Observations
What impact did the service have in the community?	Self-reflective tools (e.g., journals)
What decisions do you want to make about the program in the future?	Pre-/post-service assessments on key indicators, such as grades, attendance, discipline referrals, school climate, etc.

School psychologists and counselors are familiar with basic measurement procedures of collecting baseline data (preintervention), implementing the intervention, then collecting postintervention data to determine the effects. Service-learning processes and outcomes can be assessed through surveys and rating scales, direct observation, interviews, school records, or permanent products of reflection and service activities. Surveys and rating scales are indirect measures that record the perceptions, and possibly, the imprecise memories of the respondent. These tools are most useful when the respondent is very familiar with the information requested contained on the survey or scale. Systematic direct observation can provide valuable data about students' time on task or performance during service learning; however, data collection can be staff intensive and can only capture a small sample of the event. Interviews are useful to gather impressions from participants about their service-learning experiences that may be investigated further. School records are a source of important assessment data (e.g., curriculum-based measurement [CBM], grades, test scores, attendance, tardiness, discipline referrals). Permanent products, such as work samples and service-learning reflections, can be assembled into student portfolios. Because of the different advantages and limitations of each strategy, multimethod approaches are recommended.

The Compendium of Assessment and Research Tools (CART) is a database maintained by RMC Research Corporation in Denver (see http://www.rmcdenver.com). CART includes descriptions of research instruments, rubrics, and guidebooks for studying the effectiveness of service learning. Also included are copies of instruments, reliability and validity data, and information on the populations for which the instruments were designed. The database is organized according to three categories of variables: The *design and implementation* domain reflects program components and factors that directly affect how the program is implemented. The *context* domain represents factors indirectly related to the implementation of service learning such as school and community contexts. The *outcome* domain is organized to reflect the area where change would be expected to occur as the result of service learning, including personal, social, career, and academic factors.

The Search Institute (2000) is the primary resource for assessing service-learning outcomes through an asset-building lens. Their guidebook (pp. 110–119) contains assessment tools addressing the eight categories of developmental assets that are connected to service learning, for example:

1. Support: In what way did you feel supported by family/school/peers during your service-learning project?
2. Empowerment: How did your service make you feel that you were making a difference?
3. Boundaries and Expectations: Who were positive role models during your service experience?
4. Constructive Use of Time: How did your service experience make you want to be more involved in school?
5. Commitment to Learning: How did this experience make you want to continue your education?
6. Positive Values: What kinds of positive values were reinforced during your service experience?
7. Social Competencies: What did you learn about getting along with others?
8. Positive Identity: How did the service experience make you feel good about yourself and your future?

Students also can engage in evaluation as part of their service-learning experience. First, they can conduct a community needs assessment to help set the agenda for a service-learning project. They can evaluate the implementation plan and record the impact of various activities on the recipients of service. Evaluating their own work reinforces the students' ownership of the service project. Alternatively, students can function as "outside" evaluators as a service activity by interviewing or observing the recipients of service, analyzing the data, and reporting the results (Campbell, Edgar, & Halstead, 1994).

Evaluation should be viewed as an integral part of every implementation plan. Research and evaluation are vitally important not only to the entire educational community but to the daily work of school psychologists and counselors in ensuring that their interventions positively impact students. Service learning can achieve the goals of NCLB by providing the positive experiences needed to produce resilient students. In using service learning as an intervention, there will be a need to answer the question: Was the service-learning intervention effective in promoting the developmental assets needed for healthy social, emotional, career, and academic development and resiliency?

References

Batsche, G., Elliot, J., Graden, J.L., Grimes, J., Kovaleski, J.F., Prasse, D., et al. (2005). *Response to intervention: Policy considerations and implementation*. Alexandria, VA: National Association of State Directors of Special Education.

Berman, S.H. (August, 2000). Service as systemic reform. *School Administrator, 57*(7), 20–24.

Billig, S.H., & Eyler, J. (Eds.). (2002). *Deconstructing service learning: Research exploring context, participation, and impacts.* Greenwich, CT: Information Age Publishing.

Bradley, L.R. (1996). Evaluation helps programs function better. In G. Gulati-Partee & W.R. Finger (Eds.), *Critical issues in K-12 service-learning* (pp. 97–102). Raleigh, NC: National Society for Experiential Education.

Campbell, P., Edgar, S., & Halstead, A. (1994). Students as evaluators: A model for program evaluation. *Phi Delta Kappan, 76,* 160–165.

Cruz, N.I., & Giles, D.E. (2000). Where's the community in service-learning research? *Michigan Journal of Community Service-Learning, 7,* 28–34.

Duckenfield, M., & Drew, S. (2006). Measure what matters and no child will be left behind. In *Growing to greatness: The state of service-learning project* (pp. 33–39). St. Paul, MN: National Youth Leadership Council.

Duckenfield, M., & Swanson, L. (1992). *Service-learning: Meeting the needs of youth at risk.* Clemson University: National Dropout Prevention Center.

Elias, M.J., Zins, J.E., Graczyk, P.A., & Weissberg, R.P. (2003). Implementation, sustainability, and scaling up of social–emotional and academic innovations in public schools. *School Psychology Review, 12,* 303–319.

Gresham, F.M. (1991). Conceptualizing behavior disorders in terms of resistance to intervention. *School Psychology Review, 20,* 23–36.

Gresham, F.M. (2002). Responsiveness to intervention: The next step in special education identification, service, and exiting decision-making. In R. Bradley, L. Danielson, & D. Hallahan (Eds.), *Learning disabilities: Research to practice* (pp. 531–547). Mahwah, NJ: Lawrence Erlbaum.

Gresham, F.M. (2004). Current status and future directions of school-based behavioral interventions. *School Psychology Review, 33,* 326–343.

Institute for Global Education and Service-Learning. (2003a). *Elements of effective service learning.* Levittown, PA: Author. Retrieved June 8, 2006, from http://www.igesl.org/Understanding_service-learning_113004.pdf.

Institute for Global Education and Service-Learning. (2003b). *High quality service-learning checklist.* Levittown, PA: Author.

Kielsmeier, J.C., Scales, P.C., Roehlkepartain, E.C., & Neal, M. (2004). Community service and service-learning is public schools. *Growing to greatness: The state of service-learning project* (pp. 6–11). St. Paul, MN: National Youth Leadership Council.

Lewis, A.C. (2003). New hope for educational research? *Phi Delta Kappan, 84,* 339–340.

McNamara, K., & Hollinger, C. (2003). Intervention-based assessment: Evaluation rates and eligibility findings. *Exceptional Children, 69,* 181–183.

Middle, W. (1998). *Igniting the flame: Establishing a service-learning task force.* Clemson University, South Carolina: National Dropout Prevention Center.

Muscott, H.S. (2001, Spring). An introduction to service-learning for students with emotional and behavioral disorders: Answers to frequently asked questions. *Beyond Behavior, 10*(3), 8–15.

No Child Left Behind Act. (2001). Pub. L. No. 107–110.

Pritchard, F.F., & Whitehead, G.I. (2004). *Serve and learn: Implementing and evaluating service-learning in middle and high schools.* Mahwah, NJ: Lawrence Erlbaum.

Rockwell, S. (2001, Spring). Service-learning: Barriers, benefits, and models of excellence. *Beyond Behavior, 10*(3), 16–21.

Search Institute. (2000). *An asset builder's guide to service-learning.* Minneapolis, MN: Author.

Shumer, R. (October, 1997). What research tells us about designing service learning programs. *NASSP Bulletin, 81,* 18–24.

Smink, J., & Duckenfield, M. (1998). *Making the case for service-learning action research and evaluation.* St. Paul, MN: National Youth Leadership Council.

4
Administrative Issues

Ethical Issues

As service learning moves into the mainstream of educational practices, it is inevitable that ethical challenges will surface in using the community as a classroom. Therefore, it is critical that school psychologists and counselors have an understanding of the cultural contexts in which they work and a clear sense of their ethical responsibilities to the community (Houser, Wilczenski, & Ham, 2006). First and foremost, the needs of the students have to be balanced with those of the community to ensure equal benefits. Service learning should not stigmatize or impose a burden on the community in any way (Quinn, Gamble, & Denham, 2001).

Service learning always involves multiple constituencies—students, school staff, administrators, and community members. Community agencies are bound to follow the codes of ethics or agency policies for professional conduct within their own disciplines or facilities. Chapdelaine, Ruiz, Warchal, and Wells (2005, pp. 17–19) have proposed a code of ethics for service learning in higher education. Several codes are adapted here as they also apply to service learning in K-12 settings. The student codes provide guidelines for behavior and decision making. Students shall:

- understand their role and its limitations in the context of the assignment,
- adhere to the policies and procedures of the community agency,
- treat service recipients with respect,
- maintain confidentiality as appropriate to the situation,
- fulfill their service-learning commitments as assigned,
- reflect upon potential challenges to their personal value system,
- ask the supervisor for assistance when unsure of proper procedures, and
- consult with staff if any aspect of the service-learning assignment causes undue distress.

Ethical codes for staff not only reflect best practices in service learning but are also professional obligations. Staff shall:

- match community needs with service-learning goals to ensure that the goals are achievable,
- minimize potential harm to community agencies,
- provide community agencies with a plan of what is expected of students and the agency,
- clearly communicate goals and objectives of service learning to students,
- properly prepare students for their roles in the service-learning activities,
- ensure that students understand the diverse characteristics of those with whom they will be working,
- maintain involvement with the community agency throughout the project,
- be available to students for problem solving and conflict resolution, and
- assess the outcomes of the project for the students, recipients, and community.

In preparing responsible citizens, administrators also have a responsibility to support service learning as a legitimate way to deliver school curriculum. Administrators shall:

- be sensitive and knowledgeable about community needs,
- make effort to minimize risks and ensure safety at service-learning sites,
- provide guidelines concerning liability and ethical issues,
- provide professional development opportunities in service learning, and
- provide mechanisms for the sustainability of service-learning programs.

Although not a profession in itself, service learning can present unique issues because of complex school and community relationships. A code of conduct for service learning is needed to remind all those involved of appropriate roles, responsibilities, and behaviors.

Legal Issues

This section is not intended to be a thorough review of laws pertaining to service learning or to take the place of legal advice and consultation. It is a review of common legal issues that might arise when combining service and learning.

Community service, both voluntary and mandatory, is rapidly expanding in US schools (McLellan & Youniss, 2003). During the 1990s, two federal laws were passed to support community service: The National and Community Service Act of 1990, signed by former President George H. Bush, provides financial support for primary, secondary, and postsecondary institutions that offer community service, and the National Service Trust Act of 1993, passed during the Clinton administration, offers financial assistance to adolescents at least 16 years of age who participate in service.

Mandatory Service Programs

Increasing funds for service programs, coupled with increasing educational research supporting service, have resulted in increasing implementation of service learning. Along with this expansion, a trend from voluntary to required service went unchallenged until some school districts began to adopt mandatory service requirements as a prerequisite for high school graduation (Education Commission of the States, 1999; Johnson & Notah, 1999). The move to make graduation contingent on service has met with resistance. The argument is that mandatory community service is a violation of the 13th amendment of the Constitution, which prohibits involuntary servitude (Seidman & Tremper, 1994). None of the legal challenges have been successful:

- Steirer v. Bethlehem Area School District (1993)
- Immediato v. Rye Neck School District (1995)
- Herndon v. Chapel Hill-Carrboro City Board of Education (1996)

In each of the three cases, the federal courts upheld requirements for student service as a prerequisite for high school graduation. Johnson and Notah summarized the four arguments made by the courts to support their rulings:

- Service does not entail the type of conduct for which the 13th amendment provides protection.
- Service programs provide a public service that is not under the auspices of the 13th amendment.
- Mandatory service serves an educational purpose and therefore cannot constitute servitude.
- Community service participation is voluntary because the student is not bound to attend that school and participate in its programs.

Child Labor Laws

Goldstein (1990) suggested that mandatory service learning is parallel to working for pay. Seidman and Tremper (1994) indicated that if service is more like work than education, work-related laws may apply (e.g., minimum wage). Furthermore, if a student's service replaces a paid employee, employment protections must be considered. True student "volunteers" are exempt from federal wage and child labor laws. However, Seidman and Tremper pointed out that the definition of a "volunteer" is sometimes vague and if there is any question, it is best to check with your state department of labor regarding standards for service performed by minors.

Anti-discrimination Laws

Service-learning programs that receive federal aid are subject to federal nondiscrimination laws (Seidman & Tremper, 1994). These laws may also prevent students from being placed in agencies that engage in discriminatory practices. Schools can arrange placements based on academic achievement, but those academic standards should not have the effect of excluding a disproportionate number of students from a particular race or ethnic background.

Logistic and Liability Issues

Logistical issues are important considerations when preparing a service-learning project. However, each service-learning project is unique in addressing specific community needs, and therefore, the logistics will depend on the nature and scope of the project.

The first step is to identify a meaningful and useful project. A needs assessment will help to determine what types of service will benefit the community and what students can learn from that type of service. Students should be enlisted to brainstorm the possibilities.

The next step is to plan the project, considering the following logistic issues:

• personal, social, career and academic learning goals,
• student and community members roles,
• preservice training needs of students and community members,
• project timeline,
• activity schedules,
• supervision,
• transportation,
• risk management,
• budget,
• media coverage,
• reflection time,
• project evaluation, and
• celebration of achievements.

To avoid legal liability, risk management needs to be considered prior to starting any service-learning project (Seidman & Tremper, 1994; Wright, 2003). In assessing risk, there are three essential questions:

1. What are the risks to students in performing the service?
2. What are the risks to students traveling to and from the service site?
3. What are the risks to the community agency in having students at their site?

Seidman and Tremper pointed out that the courts have generally agreed that elementary and secondary schools, and consequently, K-12 service-learning programs, must provide a high degree of custodial care for their students, and the younger the student, the greater the responsibility for the safety and welfare of the child. Schools are expected to enforce rules to protect children and to anticipate and avert potentially harmful student behavior. Furthermore, a service site, such as a community agency, must also exercise care in protecting children from harm (Herman & Jackson, 2004). Depending on the nature of the service activity, it would be prudent to obtain a background screening check for adults in the community who are assigned to work closely with students.

Most schools have risk management procedures in place for field trips, threats of violence, accidents, and so on. Consult administrators about the school's liability requirements for permission slips, adult supervision, emergency contact information for students, and driver's insurance for those providing transportation. The school's business manager can check insurance policies for exclusions against the service-learning project, especially if activities are to be conducted off school grounds. The school's legal counsel may be asked to review consent forms designed to limit liability.

In addition to those existing procedures, Seidman and Tremper (1994) recommended the following supplementary guidelines designed specifically for service-learning programs.

- Be sure all participants (students, faculty, supervisors, community agents) know what is expected of them.
- Be sure everyone has been properly trained and equipped to perform the service competently and safely.
- Be sure everyone knows how to report problems and suggest solutions.

The ultimate goal in identifying and assessing potential risks is to prevent the occurrence of adverse events. The safety of the students as well as the recipients of their service should be the top priority. It is not only financial losses that are at stake, but also the loss of trust and misunderstandings in school–community relationships. Both effective service-learning programs and risk management procedures require careful planning and common sense. Good risk management is synonymous with good program management and ethical practice (Chapdelaine et al., 2005).

Funding

In general, service learning is extremely cost-effective. Service-learning projects carried out within the school itself usually have little or no additional costs. Depending on the type of service-learning project, revenue may be needed for professional staff development, transportation to community sites, or materials and equipment. Burt (1999) prepared a useful booklet identifying potential funding sources for service-learning projects as well as tips on grant writing.

There are several quick and easy sources to find money or supplies through local businesses or organizations (Wright, 2003). Keep in mind that students often get better results than do adults when they make the appeal for funds. Simply write up a proposal describing your project needs and submit it to the manager. For example, you might try the following sources:

- Food:

  Fast food restaurants
  Coffee shops

- Building supplies:

  Hardware stores

- Trees and plants:

  Local nurseries
  National Gardening Association (http://www.garden.org)
  National Tree Trust (http://www.nationaltreetrust.org)

- Merchant fundraising:

  Kohl's Kids Who Care
  (http://www.kohlscorporation.com/CommunityRelations/Community06.htm)

- Merchant grants:

  Starbucks
    (http://www.Starbucks.com/aboutus/foundation.asp)

Other potential funding opportunities include:

- Federal grants such as Learn and Serve America
- State grants available through the Department of Education
- Philanthropic foundations listed in local libraries
- Partnerships with local business and community-based organizations
- Parent–teacher organizations or booster clubs
- Local service organizations such as Rotary or Kiwanis
- Student-sponsored fundraisers such as car washes
- Selling products of youth service such as books of oral histories or recipes obtained during visits to a local senior center
- Appeals to alumni

Each potential funding source has advantages and disadvantages. Larger sums of money are obtainable through federal programs; however, the application process is likely to be complex and the project may need to be an innovation that will serve as a model. Funding applications for state level initiatives are less complex, but the project will probably need to fit the Department of Education priorities.

Philanthropic foundation grant applications are often brief, perhaps just a letter of application, but less money is available and the grants are generally short-term. Grant applications for corporations are also informal but it is sometimes difficult to identify specific corporate contacts for funding. Organizations and clubs may require a presentation of the planned project at one of their meetings, and there is usually less money available than previously mentioned in sources. Local businesses sometimes support school projects but the availability of this source of funding is typically made known through word-of-mouth contacts and may be time-consuming to identify. Student fundraising builds school and community spirit but it can also take considerable time and effort. Securing financial help from alumni or other individuals in the community can get a project started and may be a source of continued funding, but it takes time to identify, contact, and solicit funds from those potential supporters. Once you can demonstrate benefits of integrating service learning into the curriculum, administrators can make the case for incorporating it into the school budget.

There are many resources about writing successful grants (e.g., Burt, 1999; Gajda & Tulikangas, 2005; Levenson, 2001; Pomeroy, 1994). The basic components of a proposal include:

- Title page: Name the project and provide contact information.
- Summary: Provide a two- or three-paragraph overview of the entire project.
- Introduction: Describe the need for the project and the amount of money requested.
- Problem statement: Define the specific problem and identify your target population.
- Goals and objectives: State what the project intends to do.
- Project description: Give details of the plan to accomplish your goals and objectives, including the timeline and key personnel.
- Evaluation: Explain how you will determine the impact of the project.
- Future funding: Discuss how the project will be sustained when the initial funding terminates.
- Budget: List expenses and include in-kind contributions in detail.
- Appendix: Include material that was referenced in the body of the proposal.

In writing your proposal, follow the guidelines provided by the funding agency. Be sure to have a clear and positively stated idea. Link the idea to current trends and practices in service learning. Generalities or emotional terms can weaken the argument. Provide statistics or other types of data to back up the statement of need. Be realistic about what can be reasonably accomplished through the project. Outline a step-by-step plan to carry out and evaluate the impact of the project. Do not give the impression that money alone will solve the problem. Sending a letter to an agency to inquire about its priorities may be helpful, but do not ask a potential funding source to read a draft of the proposal.

These administrative concerns are common to many school programs and educational innovations and are likely to increase with more complex service-learning projects. But logistical issues are not insurmountable and given the potential benefits of service learning are well worth the effort.

References

Burt, V.J. (1999). *Digging for buried treasure: Finding funding for the future in service-learning.* Clemson University: National Dropout Prevention Center.

Chapdelaine, A., Ruiz, A., Warchal, J., & Wells, C. (2005). *Service-learning code of ethics.* Bolton, MA: Anker Publishing.

Education Commission of the States. (1999). *Mandatory community service: Citizenship education or involuntary servitude?* Denver, CO: Author.

Gajda, R., & Tulikangas, R. (2005). *Getting the grant: How educators can write winning proposals and manage successful projects.* Alexandria, VA: Association for Supervision and Curriculum Development.

Goldstein, M.B. (1990). Legal issues in combining service and learning. In J.C. Kendall (Ed.), *Combining service and learning: A resource book for community and public service, Vol. II* (pp. 39–60). Raleigh, NC: National Society for Experiential Education.

Herman, M.L., & Jackson, P.M. (2004). *No surprises: Harmonizing risk and reward in volunteer management.* Washington, DC: Nonprofit Risk Management Section.

Houser, R., Wilczenski, F.L., & Ham, M. (2006). *Culturally relevant ethical decision-making in counseling.* Thousand Oaks, CA: SAGE Publications.

Johnson, A.M., & Notah, D.J. (1999). Service-learning: History, literature review, and a pilot study of eighth graders. *Elementary School Journal, 99,* 453–467.

Levenson, S. (2001). *How to get grants and gifts for the public schools.* Boston: Allyn & Bacon.

McLellan, J.A., & Youniss, J. (2003). Two systems of youth service: Determinants of voluntary and required youth community service. *Journal of Youth and Adolescence, 32,* 47–58.

Pomeroy, J. (1994). *How to write a mini-grant proposal.* Freeport, NY: Educational Activities.

Quinn, S.C., Gamble, D., & Denham, A. (2001). Ethics and community-based education: Balancing respect for the community with professional preparation. *Family Community Health, 23*(4), 9–23.

Seidman, A., & Tremper, C. (1994). *Legal issues for service-learning programs.* Washington, DC: Nonprofit Risk Management Center.

Wright, J. (2003). *Administrator's guide to service-learning.* Clemson University: National Dropout Prevention Center.

5
Changing Roles and the Process of Changing

Role Changes

Service learning is a critical link to integrate the work of mental health professionals with the academic mission of schools. Service learning is synergetic in promoting positive social and emotional development as well as in enabling academic growth by providing situations in the community where caring, helping, collaboration, and sensitivity to culture become integral parts of the educative process (Billig, 2004). Data confirming the relationship between service-learning and positive social, emotional, and academic outcomes are sufficient evidence that mental health professionals, together with classroom teachers and community members, should strive to make service learning a vital part of the school curriculum. Through service-learning opportunities within communities, students learn in an authentic context and gain a sense of purpose in affecting their environment (Damon, Menon, & Bronk, 2003).

The National Association of School Psychologists (NASP, 2000), the American School Counselor Association (ASCA, 2003), and the School Social Work Association of America (SSWAA, 2003) recognize that school-based mental health services for the 21st century will be characterized by strong community–school partnerships. In addition, these organizations recommended transformations in school-based mental health service delivery to emphasize positive, ecological, proactive, multidisciplinary, and systemic practice in order to promote resiliency and build academic competencies for all children.

Still, changes have been slow to occur. Among the hindrances to school change are legal mandates, such as the No Child Left Behind (NCLB) Act (2001) and the Individuals with Disabilities Education Act (IDEA, 1999), bureaucratic constraints, and inflexible funding schemes. Sometimes school counselors and school psychologists face professional identity issues (Lambie & Williamson, 2004; Reschly & Ysseldyke, 2002). At a personal level, mental health professionals may be reluctant to change out of fear that new roles would jeopardize their current positions in schools. At a systems level, schools do not always have the infrastructures to support comprehensive approaches for mental health services; for example, several counselors and psychologists may practice independently within a school or a school district even though they are focused on related social and emotional matters.

If teachers and principals view the work of school psychologists and school counselors as ancillary, specialized tasks that are marginal to the academic mission of schools, instead of as an essential component of student achievement, then there is a great risk to the sustainability of mental health services in schools. However, there is evidence of recent shifts in the perceptions of mental health professionals as educational leaders and social change agents (Clark & Stone, 2000; DeVoss & Andrews, 2006; House & Hayes, 2002). School-based mental health professionals need to deal with problems and issues that have fueled public concerns about the state of education in the United States and, further, to identify themselves as education service providers.

Interventions introduced by school psychologists and counselors to enhance social and emotional learning are often not aligned with the mission for which schools are held primarily accountable, that is, academic achievement. However, coordinated social, emotional, and academic learning programming should be fundamental to preschool through high school education (Greenberg et al., 2003), and service learning can be the tie that binds all of these together. Service learning provides authentic learning contexts. Through service learning, school psychologists and school counselors can coordinate social, emotional, and academic learning objectives to simultaneously improve students' social and emotional functioning and academic achievement (Wilczenski & Coomey, in press, 2008; Wilczenski & Schumacher, 2006).

Restructuring Mental Health Services in Schools

Adelman and Taylor (1999, 2000) introduced the concept of an enabling component to restructure mental health services. As an academic enabling activity, school mental health practices should be fully integrated in the instructional and management components of schools. Social and emotional competence enabling academic competence would then be seen as an integral part of the school curriculum. This restructuring moves mental health services from the margins to the center of school reform efforts. Adelman and Taylor recommended redeploying staff as change agents by establishing resource-coordinating teams in schools to function as system-wide steering committees. Resource-oriented teams differ from the types of teams that schools currently use to review individual students. Instead, teachers, school psychologists, and school counselors would coordinate programs to achieve their mutual goals of social, emotional, and academic competence (Elias, Zins, Graczyk, & Weissberg, 2003; Greenberg et al., 2003). Resource-coordinating teams would provide a mechanism to weave together school and community resources to function in a cohesive way to support social, emotional, and academic development through service learning. These desired outcomes could be accomplished through flexible roles and functions. The table below suggests new roles and functions connecting the work of administrators, teachers, and mental health professionals in schools.

Connecting Mental Health Professionals and Educators in Service learning

Educational Administrators' Responsibilities	Teachers' Responsibilities	Shared Responsibilities	Mental Health Professionals' Responsibilities
Evaluate past efforts and identify current system needs	Identify student needs	Define goals	Create assessment tools, eg, formative and summative evaluations
Provide opportunity for professional development in-service	Participate in professional development in-service	Accept service-learning strategies	Conduct service-learning professional development in-service
Convene curriculum committee	Participate in curriculum development	Establish collaborative relationships	Participate in curriculum development
Facilitate community contacts	Create academic curriculum	Integrate social, emotional, and academic curricula	Create social and emotional curriculum
Facilitate school/community partnerships	Begin community experiences	Ensure appropriate supervision in community	Arrange service schedules
Recognize importance of reflection in learning	Provide opportunities for students' to reflect upon social, emotional, ethical and academic learning	Compile data on student reflection	Provide opportunities for students' to reflect upon social, emotional, ethical and academic learning
Provide opportunities for faculty meetings	Reflect upon service-learning experiences	Compile data on professional self-reflections	Reflect upon service-learning experiences
Work with state and local boards of education to establish service-learning curriculum requirements	Measure and evaluate SL academic outcomes	Determine effective components of service learning	Measure and evaluate service-learning social and emotional outcomes
Provide faculty incentives for service	Evaluate community impact	Recognize student achievement	Evaluate community impact

Change Processes

Using service learning to meet personal, social, career, and academic goals for students will probably be easier for some mental health professionals than for others. What is the difference between those who find implementing innovations easy and those who do not? It is likely that they differ in how they see themselves and their work. If a professional has always felt effective in working with students through traditional service delivery including assessment, individual and group counseling, and parent and teacher consultation, then what is the imperative to change? NCLB has made this a different world! Now, there is an emphasis on demonstrating how school programs contribute to student academic achievement. School-based mental health professionals can clearly link social/emotional learning with academic learning through service learning. School psychologists and school counselors need to refocus their concerns away from service delivery (what do we do?) to a concern with student competency (how are students different because of what we do?).

Systemic changes require new ways of thinking and functioning for school psychologists and school counselors including those related to the change process itself. Recent professional literature in school psychology (Schaughency & Ervin, 2006; Strein, Hoagwood, & Cohn, 2003) and school counseling (Keys, 1999; Stone & Dahir, 2006) addresses how to promote and sustain school change. Sarason (1982, p. 78) cautioned: "You can have the most creative, compellingly valid, educationally productive idea in the world, but whether it can become embedded and sustained in a socially complex setting will be primarily a function of how you conceptualize the implementation-change process." Service learning involves change. Therefore, it is important for mental health professionals to understand the process of change in schools and to support individuals and organizations as the change process evolves.

Hall and Hord (1987, 2001) proposed the Concerns-Based Adoption Model (CBAM), which is a widely applied and empirically grounded theory and methodology for studying the process of implementing change in schools (Anderson, 1997). Hall and Hord developed the model to study organizationally focused innovations, making it a potentially useful framework to examine changing roles for school-based mental health professionals and to monitor the implementation of service-learning interventions. One component of the model focuses the stages of the implementation process itself and the other component focuses on the stages of participants' response to change as the implementation process unfolds. The model suggests that over time, people experiencing change evolve in terms of how they use innovations as well as their concerns about change.

According to Hall and Hord, an understanding of both the behavioral and the affective dimensions of change is crucial to facilitating the change process. CBAM applies to anyone experiencing change—school psychologists, counselors, teachers, administrators, students, parents, community members. Several assumptions about change support CBAM: (1) change is a process, not an event; (2) change is accomplished by individuals; (3) change is a highly personal experience; (4) change involves developmental growth in feelings and skills; and (5) change can be facilitated by interventions directed simultaneously toward individuals and organizations.

Change processes are complex and dynamic (Hord, Rutherford, Huling, & Hall, 2004). Innovations are almost always altered as they are implemented, and change will be an ever-evolving process. The major theme of CBAM is that the people affected by the change are the determining factor in the change process. There is a developmental sequence to concerns about change, typically progressing from *self-concern* (I need more information about this new idea.) to *task-concern* (Can I do this? Do I have the time for this?) to *impact-concern* (How is this affecting students? What can we do to make it better?). The impact-concerns stage restarts the cycle. Rosenfield (1992) suggested that the process of change in schools requires guidance, mutual adoption, and supportive planning over a 3- to 5-year time period. By developing an understanding of the change process, school psychologists and school counselors as consultants can patiently support the development of new roles and functions that can be smoothly integrated with the routine operations of the school (Bemak, 2000; West & Idol, 1993).

In the final analysis, the most pressing requirement for sustaining change in school practices is attention to the attitudes and beliefs of practitioners (Coburn, 2003). School psychologists, counselors, teachers, and administrators, and community members must embrace a new way of functioning and agree that service learning is in fact a preferred way to deliver a social, emotional, career, and academic curriculum. Moreover, school-based mental health professionals need to take on versatile roles as change agents to promote service learning as systemic social and emotional innovation that can be sustained by being integrated in the academic curriculum. Assuming a professional role as a change agent is compatible with new thrusts for practice in the fields of school psychology (NASP, 2000) and school counseling (ASCA, 2003).

Making service learning come alive in schools requires a fundamental shift in attitude about student development and the nature of education (Senge et al., 2000). The same is true for school-based mental health services. Certainly, school psychologists and school counselors need to be concerned with social and emotional issues, but they also need to function as educational service providers and collaborative leaders. As advocates for positive and systemic practices, school psychologists and counselors must apply what they know works best in integrating social, emotional, and academic learning to make the case for service learning with their colleagues, administrators, parents, PTAs, and school boards. School psychologists and counselors should also reflect on their own concerns about changing roles from individual to systemic work—they are part of the change process. There are many opportunities for school psychologists and counselors to focus on positive traits instead of problems by employing service learning as a strategy to integrate social and emotional education with the academic mission of schools.

References

Adelman, H.S., & Taylor, L. (1999). Reframing mental health in schools and expanding school reform. *Educational Psychologist, 33,* 135–152.

Adelman, H.S., & Taylor, L. (2000). Moving prevention from the fringes into the fabric of school improvement. *Journal of Educational and Psychological Consultation, 11,* 7–36.

American School Counselor Association [ASCA]. (2003). *The ASCA national model: A framework for school counseling programs.* Alexandria, VA: Author.

Anderson, S.E. (1997). Understanding teacher change: Revisiting the concerns based adoption model. *Curriculum Inquiry, 27,* 331–367.

Bemak, F. (2000). Transforming the role of the counselor to provide leadership in educational reform through collaboration. *Professional School Counseling, 3,* 323–331.

Billig, S.H. (2004). Heads, hearts, and hands: The research on K-12 service-learning. In J. Kielsmeier, M. Neal, & M. McKinnon (Eds.), *Growing to greatness: The state of service-learning project* (pp. 12–25). St. Paul, MN: National Youth Leadership Council.

Clark, M.A., & Stone, C. (2000). The developmental school counselor as educational leader. In J. Wittmer (Ed.), *Managing your school counseling program: K-12 developmental strategies* (pp. 75–82). Minneapolis, MN: Educational Media Corporation.

Coburn, C.E. (2003). Rethinking scale: Moving beyond numbers to deep and lasting change. *Educational Researcher, 32*(6), 3–12.

Damon, W., Menon, J., & Bronk, K.C. (2003). The development of purpose during adolescence. *Applied Developmental Science, 7,* 119–128.

DeVoss, J.A., & Andrews, M.F. (2006). *School counselors as educational leaders.* Boston: Houghton-Mifflin.

Elias, M.J., Zins, J.E., Graczyk, P.A., & Weissberg, R.P. (2003). Implementation, sustainability, and scaling up of social–emotional and academic innovations in public schools. *School Psychology Review, 12,* 303–319.

Greenberg, M.T., Weissberg, R.P., O'Brien, M.U., Zins, J., Fredericks, L., Resnik, H., et al. (2003). Enhancing school-based prevention and youth development through coordinated social, emotional, and academic learning. *American Psychologist, 58,* 466–474.

Hall, G.E., & Hord, S.M. (1987). *Change in schools: Facilitating the process.* New York: State University of New York Press.

Hall, G.E., & Hord, S.M. (2001). *Implementing change: Patterns, principles, and potholes.* Boston: Allyn & Bacon.

Hord, S., Rutherford, W.L., Huling, L., & Hall, G.E. (2004). *Taking charge of change.* Austin, TX: Southwest Educational Development Laboratory.

House, R., & Hayes, R. (2002). School counselors: Becoming key players in school reform. *Professional School Counseling, 5,* 249–256.

Individuals with Disabilities Education Act [IDEA]. (1999). 34 C.F.R. 300 (Regulations), Regulations Implementing IDEA (1997). (*Federal Register.* 1999). 64(48).

Keys, S.G. (1999). The school counselor's role in facilitating multi-systemic change. *Professional School Counseling, 3,* 101–107.

Lambie, G.W., & Williamson, L.L. (2004). The challenge to change from guidance counseling to professional school counseling: An historical perspective. *Professional School Counseling, 8,* 124–131.

National Association of School Psychologists [NASP] (2000). *Guidelines for the provision of school psychological services.* Bethesda, MD: Author.

No Child Left Behind [NCLB] Act. (2001). Pub. L. No. 107–110.

Reschly, D.J., & Ysseldyke, J.E. (2002). Paradigm shift: The past is not the future. In A. Thomas & J. Grimes (Eds.), *Best practices in school psychology—IV* (pp. 3–20). Bethesda, MD: National Association of School Psychologists.

Rosenfield, S. (1992). Developing school-based consultation teams: A design for organizational change. *School Psychology Quarterly, 7,* 27–46.

Sarason, S.B. (1982). *The culture of the school and the problem of change* (2nd ed.). Boston: Allyn & Bacon.

School Social Work Association of America [SSWAA]. (2003). *SSWAA organizational mission statement.* Northlake, IL: Author.

Schaughency, E., & Ervin, R. (Eds.). (2006). Building capacity to implement and sustain effective practices. [Special issue]. *School Psychology Review, 35*(2).

Senge, P., Cambron-McCabe, N., Lucas, T., Smith, B., Dutton, J. and Kleiner, A. (2000). *Schools that learn: A fifth discipline fieldbook for educators, parents, and everyone who cares about education.* New York: Doubleday.

Stone, C.B., & Dahir, C.A. (2006). *The transformed school counselor.* Boston: Lahaska Press.

Strein, W., Hoagwood, K., & Cohn, A. (2003). School psychology: A public health perspective: Prevention, populations, and systems change. *Journal of School Psychology, 41,* 23–38.

West, J.F., & Idol, L. (1993). The counselor as consultant in the collaborative school. *Journal of Counseling and Development, 71,* 678–683.

Wilczenski, F.L., & Coomey, S.M. (in press, 2008). Best practices in service-learning: Enhancing both the social/emotional and academic competence of all students. In Thomas & J. Grimes (Eds.), *Best practices in school psychology—V.* Bethesda, MD: National Association of School Psychologists.

Wilczenski, F.L., & Schumacher, R.A. (2006). Giving and growing: Service learning applications in school counseling. *School Counselor, 43*(4), 58–63.

6
Service Learning in Professional Education and Development

Service learning is prominent in higher education (Campus Compact, 2004; Jacoby, 1996) and, in particular, in teacher education (Anderson, Swick, & Yff, 2001; Boyle-Baise, 2002). There are a variety of reasons for integrating service learning in professional education and development for school psychologists and school counselors. The next generation of mental health professionals must be prepared to function in the schools of today as well as be prepared to take a leadership role in improving schools for the future (Adelman & Taylor, 1999, 2000; Greenberg et al., 2003).

It is imperative that those who prepare school psychologists and school counselors seek strategies for multicultural learning experiences with diverse student populations in diverse community settings. In addition, wellness promotion and positive approaches to youth development need to be stressed in graduate education. Community psychology is a relevant knowledge base because it focuses on social issues and institutions, such as schools, that influence community functioning. School psychologists and school counselors also need to be prepared for versatile roles as change agents and should be provided with a firm grounding in theories of educational leadership. Generalist training will need to be balanced with specialized training so that school-based mental health professionals recognize the commonalities among various student problems and address them in a systemic rather than individual manner. A new kind of professional will be needed to foster sustainable, systemic social and emotional innovations that are integrated in the academic curriculum. These new professionals will need experience as educational leaders, coordinators, and organizational consultants. In this era of No Child Left Behind and accountability, school psychologists and counselors will need graduate and postdegree training in program evaluation and action research in order to measure outcomes and contribute to the evidence base concerning social, emotional, career, and academic development (Cruz & Giles, 2000; Dorado & Giles, 2004; Elias, Zins, Graczyk, & Weissberg, 2003). Service learning has the potential to meet those professional preparation goals.

Graduate preparation and continuing professional development in service learning is needed not only to introduce the concept but to assist school psychologists and school counselors to develop a deep understanding of its complexities and uses. To use service learning effectively, school psychologists and counselors must be able to identify important social, emotional, career, and academic curriculum connections to the community service project, perhaps moving from a therapist style interaction to more of an educative, coaching approach.

A number of school-based mental health training programs have incorporated service learning in their degree requirements. Graduate students study service learning as a positively oriented intervention and then experience it in their course work. References to service-learning applications in graduate education can be found in school psychology (e.g., Wilczenski, Coomey, & Ball, 2004) and school counseling (e.g., Arman & Scherer, 2002; Hayes, Dagley, & Horne, 1996). Service learning is also employed as an approach to teaching and learning in psychology (Bringle & Duffy, 1998). The American Psychological Association (APA) regularly holds sessions now on service learning at its conferences and has a website for information on service learning at the graduate level (see http://www.apa.org/ed/slce/home.html). Service learning in graduate education can augment programs of study in fundamental ways relevant to the values, ethics, and attitudes that are the basis of professional school psychology and counseling practice.

Experience with service learning can lead school psychologists and school counselors to a deeper intellectual interest and understanding of the nature of helping relationships. Service learning is compatible with the training standards set forth by the National Association of School Psychologists (NASP, 2000) and the American School Counselor Association (ASCA, 2003). Because of the potential benefits of service learning in counselor education, the Association for Counselor Education and Supervision (ACES, 1990) recommended that school counseling programs incorporate service learning into their curriculum by establishing partnerships between universities, community agencies, and public schools. The unique experiences available to graduate students through service-learning activities address the training domains of wellness promotion and home/school/community collaboration. Furthermore, multicultural education for school psychologists and school counselors centers on learning about cultural diversity, examining power relationships and inequality, and responding in a positive manner to sociocultural differences in schools and communities (Olson & Wilczenski, 1995). Service learning promotes the cultural awareness, sensitivity, and knowledge that are necessary for multicultural counseling competence (Burnett, Hamel, & Long, 2004; Burnett, Long, & Horne, 2005). Service learning has been shown to be effective in reducing negative stereotypes and increasing tolerance for diversity (Eyler & Giles, 1999).

Traditional coursework does not usually confront graduate students with situations that bring their values systems into question and present them with complex moral and political dilemmas. Therefore, it is critically important for students to examine issues of race and class in order to prevent service learning from replicating the social and economic injustices that created the need for community service in the first place (Green, 2001). This process of reflection is at the core of service learning (Connors & Seifer, 2005). Professors need to pay close attention to students' learning as they reflect on their service, prompting students to question their assumptions about communities as well as the context and consequences of their service, while respecting differences in the depth and complexity of each student's reflections (Morrissette & Gadbois, 2006).

Eyler, Giles, and Schmiede (1996) asked students to "reflect" on reflection and, using student testimony from those interviews, identified key components of effective reflection—the following four Cs:

- *Continuous*: Reflective preparation is essential to getting the most out of the service-learning experience. Reflection during service learning is directed toward problem solving. Refection after service learning focuses on evaluating the meaning of the experience, integrating old knowledge with new information, and formulating a future course of action.
- *Connected*: Reflection can be used to connect service with course work.
- *Challenging*: Reflection activities should force students to think in novel ways, to raise questions, and to solve problems.
- *Contextualized*: Reflection should be appropriate for the context of the service-learning project. Service projects included in course work lend themselves to formal, structured methods of reflection.

Through opportunities for reflection, students create meaning of their service experiences, gain an appreciation of human interactions, and look beyond surface issues to appreciate the complexity of problems. When students are frustrated by their service activities, they are learning something fundamental about the uncertainty and complexity of social issues as well as the challenges inherent in effecting social change. They come to realize that being committed to social justice and educational reform requires the ability to accept ambiguity and to critically examine the issues they face in human services. Learning occurs through cycles of service and reflection. By experiencing these cycles during service-learning projects, students hone the skills they will need to become reflective school psychologists and school counselors who engage in active inquiry on their professional practices (Schon, 1983, 1987).

Graduate professional education in school psychology and school counseling should provide students with opportunities to reflect on their actions with the ultimate goal of producing practitioners who reflect while in action. Service learning has the potential to truly enhance the education of school psychologists and school counselors in a meaningful way. Unlike volunteerism, which emphasizes service, or practica/internships, which emphasize learning, here the goals of community service and academic learning are equally important. Practicum and internship experiences in school psychology and counseling are closely supervised experiences where students are expected to practice skills learned in their professional preparation courses. They take on the role and function of the school psychologists or counselors as practiced within a particular training site. The essence of internship experiences is the interaction between an expert and a novice practitioner. Interns gain knowledge concerning school-based mental health services and how they are delivered. Service learning, however, can offer a different perspective and level of involvement than that found in internships. Through service-learning experiences, students can acquire understandings about the community context of schooling that are not routinely available as a school psychology or counseling professional-in-training.

The following two cases illustrate the use of service learning in school psychology and school counselor graduate programs. Both are pre-practicum service-learning experiences that were implemented to smooth students' transitions from the classroom to practicum and internship field placements.

Service Learning Integrated into School Psychology Training

The Massachusetts State Departments of Education and Social Services sponsor and oversee an Educational Surrogate Parent (ESP) Program to comply with the federal mandate. The Individuals with Disabilities Education Act (IDEA, 1999) requires that when a child or adolescent with a disability is a "ward of the state," an ESP must be appointed to legally represent the student as the parent participant in the special education planning process. In order to be an ESP, a volunteer must be at least 18 years of age, provide two references, pass a criminal background check, and attend a 3-hour training workshop concerning Individual Education Plan (IEP) processes conducted by the Department of Education (DOE). The DOE is ultimately responsible for the program and provides assistance to ESPs if they encounter any difficulty in managing their assigned cases.

Members of an introductory school psychology course at the University of Massachusetts Boston have the option of fulfilling pre-practicum requirements by serving as an ESP. Students agree to follow at least one case during the academic year. As ESPs for the DOE, students obtain all the rights of parents in educational matters, without financial responsibility. Typically, they review records, observe school programs, attend evaluation meetings, and approve IEPs. Because special education regulations depend heavily upon parental involvement, children and adolescents in state custody are disadvantaged when IEP meetings are delayed. The ESP Program is a mandated practice in the state to facilitate the special education process and students fulfill the need for volunteers.

The ESP Program pre-practicum option in the school psychology curriculum attaches equal weight to the service and learning components of the community experience (Sigmon, 1994). Students provide a valuable service to the community while furthering their own professional development. Children and adolescents in state custody benefit by having an educational advocate. Graduate students benefit from exposure to school situations and community resources outside of their usual practice. At IEP team meetings, the usual role of the school psychologist is to inform parents about the nature of their child's disabilities and to make recommendations for remedial intervention. As ESPs, school psychology students sit on the other side of the table and experience the parental position of receiving information from multiple sources and integrating that information to plan an appropriate educational program. Graduate students are called upon to use collaborative and interpersonal skills in a different way than is typically found in the classroom or internship. Their parental role offers a perspective on educational processes that is not available in traditional school psychology practica or internships. Support meetings and reflection activities provide a forum for student interaction and reflection around the substantive issues raised by the experience of being an ESP (see Wilczenski et al., 2004).

Service Learning Integrated into School Counselor Education

A primary role for counselors is to prepare high school students for postsecondary education—often that means help with the college application process. However, high school counselors cannot intervene to help their students once they graduate from high school and enter college. The transition from high school to college is a critical one because a new set of skills is required to negotiate a large college or university setting. Many students are not successful in obtaining a degree (Gehrman, 2006). In addition to academic skills, students entering the University for the first time need to increase their self-confidence and network with people who can support them over the next four years.

Boston NET (Network for Educational Transitions) is a partnership between the Boston Public Schools and the University of Massachusetts, Boston. Its mission is to provide assistance to high school students applying to the university and then to support them as they negotiate their first year at the university (Wilczenski, 2006). As a pre-practicum assignment, graduate students enrolled in an introductory professional school counseling course engage in service learning through the NET project. Graduate students implement an educational persistence program designed to provide social, emotional, and academic support for first year undergraduate students who graduated from high schools in Boston. School counseling graduate students meet regularly with the undergraduates as a group and are also available for one-to-one interaction and assistance—typically via e-mail. The goals are to foster a sense of community among the undergraduates, to support them in making appropriate emotional adjustments to college life, and to advise them about seeking academic assistance when necessary. NET addresses an authentic need to assist undergraduates to have a successful first year at the university.

The NET service-learning project gives school counseling graduate students the opportunity to observe undergraduates and learn what they need to be successful in college. To promote reflection, Kozol's (2005) book, *The Shame of the Nation*, is a required reading in the course. Graduate students consider

Kozol's perspectives, and reflect upon the achievement and opportunity gaps that exist for inner city high school students that may contribute to college dropouts.

This experience differs from other high school level counseling practicum or internship because it extends the view of the counselor-in-training to postsecondary education. Graduate students planning to work in K-8 settings also benefit from participation in this service-learning project by gaining a deeper understanding of the personal, social, career, and academic issues faced by students when they first enter college. The knowledge they acquire through this service-learning project helps them in their role as elementary level school counselors to start to prepare students at a young age for future postsecondary opportunities and challenges.

Through service learning, participatory and hands-on experience in a supportive environment enables the growth and development of learners of all ages, whether they are in K-8 settings finding their way in the world, high school students planning their future, undergraduates preparing to take on adult roles, graduate students taking their place in a school psychology or school counseling profession, or seasoned professionals seeking innovative ways of promoting positive development in youth.

References

Adelman, H.S., & Taylor, L. (1999). Reframing mental health in schools and expanding school reform. *Educational Psychologist, 33*, 135–152.

Adelman, H.S., & Taylor, L. (2000). Moving prevention from the fringes into the fabric of school improvement. *Journal of Educational and Psychological Consultation, 11*, 7–36.

American School Counselor Association [ASCA]. (2003). *The ASCA national model: A framework for school counseling programs*. Alexandria, VA: Author.

Anderson, J.B., Swick, K.J., & Yff, J. (Eds.). (2001). *Service-learning in teacher education: Enhancing the growth of new teachers, their students, and communities*. Washington, DC: American Association of Colleges of Teacher Education.

Arman, J.F., & Scherer, D. (2002). Service-learning in school counselor preparation: A qualitative analysis. *Journal of Humanistic Counseling, Education, and Development, 41*, 69–86.

Association for Counselor Education and Supervision [ACES]. (1990). Standards and procedures for school counselor training and certification. *Counselor Education and Supervision, 29*, 213–215.

Bringle, R.G., & Duffy, D. (Eds.). (1998). *With service in mind: Concepts and models for service-learning in psychology*. Washington, DC: American Association for Higher Education.

Boyle-Baise, M. (2002). *Multicultural service-learning: Educating teachers in diverse communities*. New York: Teachers College Press.

Burnett, J.A., Hamel, D., & Long, L.L. (2004). Service-learning in graduate counselor education: Developing multicultural counseling competency. *Journal of Multicultural Counseling and Development, 32*, 180–191.

Burnett, J.A., Long, L.L., & Horne, H.L. (2005). Service-learning for counselors: Integrating education, training, and the community. *Journal of Humanistic Counseling Education and Development, 44*, 158–167.

Campus Compact. (2004). *Service statistics: The engaged campus.* Providence, RI: Author. Retrieved May 15, 2006, from http://www.compact.org/news/stats2004/.

Connors, K., & Seifer, S.D. (September, 2005). *Reflection in higher education service-learning.* Community–Campus Partnerships for Health. Retrieved June 8, 2006, from http://servicelearning.org/resources/fact_sheets/he_facts/he_reflection/index.php?search_term=Reflection%20in%20higher%20ed.

Cruz, N.I., & Giles, D.E. (2000). Where's the community in service-learning research? *Michigan Journal of Community Service-Learning, 7,* 28–34.

Dorado, S., & Giles, D.E. (2004). Service-learning partnerships: Paths of engagement. *Michigan Journal of Community Service-Learning, 1,* 25–37.

Elias, M.J., Zins, J.E., Graczyk, P.A., & Weissberg, R.P. (2003). Implementation, sustainability, and scaling up of social–emotional and academic innovations in public schools. *School Psychology Review, 12,* 303–319.

Eyler, J., & Giles, D.E. (1999). *Where's the learning in service-learning?* San Francisco, CA: Jossey-Bass.

Eyler, J., Giles, D.E., & Schmiede, A. (1996). *A professional's guide to reflection in service learning: Student voices and reflections.* Nashville, TN: Vanderbilt University.

Gehrman, E. (2006, May). What makes kids drop out of college? Harvard University Gazette. Retrieved 6-8-06 from http://www.news.harvard.edu/gazette/2006/05.04/13-dropout.html.

Green, A.E. (2001). "But you aren't white:" Racial perceptions and service-learning. *Michigan Journal of Community Service Learning, 8,* 18–26.

Greenberg, M.T., Weissberg, R.P., O'Brien, M.U., Zins, J., Fredericks, L., Resnik, H., et al. (2003). Enhancing school-based prevention and youth development through coordinated social, emotional, and academic learning. *American Psychologist, 58,* 466–474.

Hayes, R.L., Dagley, J.C., & Horne, A.M. (1996). Restructuring school counselor education: Work in progress. *Journal of Counseling and Development, 74,* 378–384.

Individuals with Disabilities Education Act [IDEA]. (1999). 34 C.F.R. 300 (Regulations), Regulations Implementing IDEA (1997) (*Federal Register.* (1999). 64(48)).

Jacoby, B. (Ed.). (1996). *Service-learning in higher education.* San Francisco, CA: Jossey-Bass.

Kozol, J. (2005). *The shame of the nation: The restoration of apartheid schooling in America.* New York: Crown Publishers.

Morrissette, P.J., & Gadbois, S. (2006). Ethical consideration of counselor education teaching strategies. *Counseling and Values, 50,* 131–141.

National Association of School Psychologists [NASP]. (2000). *Guidelines for the provision of school psychological services.* Bethesda, MD: Author.

Olson, S.E., & Wilczenski, F.L. (1995). Multicultural issues and education relevant to school psychology practice. *School Psychology International Journal, 16,* 323–334.

Schon, D. (1983). *The reflective practitioner: How professionals think in action.* New York: Basic Books.

Schon, D. (1987). *Educating the reflective practitioner: Toward a new design for teaching and learning in the professions.* San Francisco: Jossey-Bass.

Sigmon, R.L. (1994). *Linking service with learning.* Washington, DC: Council of Independent Colleges. Available at http://www.cic.edu.

Wilczenski, F.L. (2006). *Boston NET: Network for Educational Transitions.* Unpublished manuscript.

Wilczenski, F.L., Coomey, S.M., & Ball, B.A. (2004). Service-learning as a vehicle for educating school psychologists. *School Psychology Trainers' Forum, 23*(4), 1–6, 8.

Section II
Service Learning as Intervention and Prevention

Students with disabilities, low socioeconomic status, or linguistic diversity are often the recipients of services in the school and community. Although supportive resources are essential for these students, they, themselves, are also important resources within their school community and the community at large. Service learning is an avenue for all students to participate in their community despite the various challenges they may face. Students with disabilities or other special needs can develop personal, social, career, and academic skills through the process of making valuable contributions to others.

Service learning, which integrates service with the school curriculum and structured reflection, is an effective strategy for a diverse student population because it engages multiple intelligences that offer more possibilities for learning. Students also see that their work is valued and that they can make a difference. Through service learning, students gain self-confidence and a sense of belonging in the community. Those are especially important internal and external developmental assets for students with special needs who often display low self-esteem and problematic interpersonal relationships.

Chapter 7 examines the opportunities for school psychologists and school counselors to apply service learning in their work with students who have identified special education needs. Chapter 8 explains the potential of service learning to promote mental health and reduce risk-taking behaviors. Chapter 9 presents service learning as an authentic, strength-based intervention to be used by school psychologists and counselors to promote resiliency in students at risk for school failure. Chapter 10 addresses school climate issues and describes the use of service learning in violence prevention and crisis intervention.

7
Special Education Applications

School psychologists and school counselors have the common goal of fostering the growth of well-adjusted citizens who are active members of their community. Service learning is a powerful tool to encourage growth for *all* students. Yet, students with physical, cognitive, and sensory disabilities often do not partake in service as a learning opportunity; rather, they are the recipients of service. To some extent, this is encouraged as compassion for the less fortunate within the service-learning literature itself. Indeed, students who serve people in unfortunate circumstances report that they feel better about themselves. Enhancing the self-esteem for one group, however, by devaluing another is unacceptable.

Avoid Disablism

Careful reflection is a critical first step in planning service-learning projects involving people with disabilities to avoid disablism. Disablism refers to a set of assumptions that promote the differential treatment of people because of actual or presumed disabilities (Beirne-Smith, Ittenbach, & Patton, 1998). Service projects must be arranged so that they do not convey a message that people with disabilities are childlike, victims of the disability, need to be repaired, or have a poor quality of life (Gent & Gurecka, 2001). Serving the community is a privilege that is often denied to persons with disabilities. Instead of being designed to do *for* students with disabilities, service-learning projects should be designed to do *with* students with disabilities. Because of its inherent flexibility and its functional application to real-life situations, service learning holds great potential to make all students valued members of the community (Gent & Gurecka, 2002). Gent and Gurecka suggested that for students with disabilities, the goal of service learning needs to be changed from an emphasis on charity to a more inclusive emphasis on relationships and on the equal participation of all parties. Relationship and participatory orientations eliminate the negative side effects of service learning—the sense of superiority for the servers and the "blame the victim" mentality toward those served. Disablism in service-learning projects can be eliminated by integrating service learning in Individual Educational Plans (IEPs) so that students with disabilities are *partners* in providing service. Once young people with disabilities contribute in meaningful ways to their communities, a change in attitudes within those communities is more likely to occur.

Service Learning for Students with Physical, Cognitive, and Sensory Disabilities

What does the literature say about service learning for students with mild, moderate, and severe disabilities? Brill (1994) surveyed special educators whose students with mild disabilities were engaged in service learning and found increases in attendance, academic skills, and socialization with nondisabled peers. Increases in self-esteem, self-knowledge, communication, and interpersonal skills were described by Yoder, Retish, and Wade (1996) for students with learning disabilities, those with limited English-speaking proficiency, and general education students involved in an inclusive service-learning program. Jennings (2001) reported gains in self-confidence for a group of middle school special education students with learning disabilities who read picture books to kindergarteners. Websites for the National Service-Learning Clearinghouse, Students in Service to America, and the National Service Inclusion Project (NSIP) identify other benefits of service learning for students with disabilities including greater attachment to school, more opportunities for career exploration, and a stronger sense of community.

Fewer research studies focus on service learning for students with moderate and severe disabilities. In a study reported by Burns, Storey, and Certo (1999), high school students with severe disabilities and students without disabilities worked together as peers in an inclusive service-learning project. At the conclusion of the service activity, peers without disabilities demonstrated more positive attitudes toward students with severe disabilities than at the start of the project. In contrast, high school students who engaged in service directed solely to *helping* students with disabilities did not evidence significant changes in attitudes.

Accommodations for Students with Disabilities

Gardner's (1983, 2000) theory of "multiple intelligences" is a powerful framework for service learning (Berman, 1999; Klopp, Toole, & Toole, 2001; Neal & Holland, 2005). Service learning offers a context in which to implement Gardner's ideas and to address the needs of student with disabilities in diverse ways that capitalizes on their strengths. Because multiple intelligences can encompass a broad range of strengths and interests (i.e., verbal/linguistic, logical/

mathematical, musical/rhythmic, visual/spatial, interpersonal, intrapersonal, bodily/kinesthetic, and naturalist), students with disabilities have greater chances for success as more types of intelligence are recognized and valued. Gardner built his theory on the intelligence required in the real world. Students with disabilities who have seldom felt successful in the classroom may experience a sense of competence in applying their knowledge and skills in authentic contexts.

Principles of universal design should be employed when planning and implementing service-learning activities (NSIP, 2003). Universal design means that rather than designing service learning for the average student, the service is designed for students with a broad range of abilities, disabilities, reading levels, and learning styles. Applied to service learning, universal design does not mean the same experience for everyone but rather it underscores the importance of exploiting the varied aspects of a service activity to meet the needs of diverse learners. Through service opportunities, students with disabilities can be given multiple ways to engage their interests, acquire knowledge, and demonstrate what they know. A service-learning project also provides a context for interdisciplinary collaboration. School psychologists and counselors can work with other disciplines and therapists (speech, language, occupational, physical) to coordinate and reinforce IEP goals and objectives. When planning service learning, it is important to remember to:

- conduct activities in accessible locations,
- provide adequate space for assistive devices, such as wheelchairs, and
- organize materials so that they can be easily identified and reached.

Service learning is starting to be infused into special and/or inclusive education programs (Kluth, 2000; Service-Learning Network, 2002). The National Service-Learning Clearinghouse is a repository of many service-learning curriculum guides and inclusive project ideas for students with disabilities. For example, *Project SUCCESS* (Morales, 1999) pairs students with and without disabilities to research and address community needs. *Yes I Can* (Institute for Community Integration, 1999) is a project designed for junior and senior high students to work together in serving their communities. *Inclusive service-learning: A training guide for K-12 teachers* (Hampshire Educational Collaborative, 2003) provides information for including students with disabilities in service-learning activities. Maryland requires service learning for graduation and their State Department of Education Student Service Alliance (Maryland Student Service Alliance, 1993) has prepared a *Service-Learning Special Education Guide* that contains service-learning project ideas for students with disabilities and tips for adapting those projects to accommodate various special needs. Adaptations for inclusive service learning may involve modifying rules for participation or breaking activities into smaller steps. The following table lists possible strategies for adapting service-learning projects to meet the special needs of students with disabilities.

General strategies for adapting service-learning projects for students with disabilities

Disability	Adaptations
Cognitive Impairment	• Design hands-on activities • Plan short blocks of time • Pair with a buddy
Specific Learning Disability	• Use multi-modal strategies • Delineate expectations clearly • Minimize written work
Emotional and Behavioral Impairments	• Allow students to make decisions • Use small groups • Provide high degree of structure
Physical and Health Impairments	• Consider partial participation • Take frequent breaks • Ensure accessibility, adapt equipment
Attention Deficit/Hyperactivity	• Design short, structured tasks • Alternate activities frequently • Pair with other students
Sensory Impairment: Blind	• Determine need for Braille • Watch for obstructions • Pair with a buddy
Sensory Impairment: Deaf	• Develop emergency signals • Accompany directions with signs • Pair with a buddy

Individualized Educational Plans

Despite its adaptability, service-learning activities are rarely included in Individualized Educational Plans (IEPs). Yet a strong case for incorporating service-learning activities into IEPs can be made by referring to the language of the Individuals with Disabilities Education Improvement Act (IDEA) of 2004, which aligns closely with the No Child Left Behind (NCLB) Act of 2001, to ensure equity, accountability, and excellence in education for students with disabilities. That legislation specifically states that students should be given opportunities to experience applied learning within the community, to access various community educational resources, to engage in career exploration, and to develop the skills necessary to meet the challenges of adulthood. Inclusive service learning is an avenue for integrating students with disabilities in the least restrictive environment (LRE). Students without disabilities have an opportunity to acquire a greater understanding of the disability issues as well as a sense of how to accommodate for students' with special needs. Schools, families, and communities must work together to offer students with disabilities appropriate involvement and progress in the general curriculum as well as preparation for postsecondary education, employment, and/or independent living.

Service learning can meet many of the IEP goals and state education standards for students with disabilities (Kleinert et al., 2004; NSIP, n.d.). When constructing IEPs:

1. Make sure that service-learning skills are an extension of educational goals and objectives.
2. Link the service activities to the evidence of learning required for the state's alternate educational assessment under IDEA.

For example, service learning allows students to document:

- that they can apply what they have learned in the classroom to other settings,
- social interaction and collaborative group skills, and
- skills such as planning a project and monitoring and evaluating success.

Mental health professionals are often involved in special education planning for students with disabilities preparing for school to work transitions at age 22. Service learning can meet various goals and objectives for vocational training and independent living while encouraging community participation. The following is an example of integrating service learning in an IEP:

Service Learning for School to Work Transitions

ADULT GOAL: To be a social worker or activity director working with elderly persons in nursing homes.

PRESENT LEVEL OF PERFORMANCE: Reading and math skills are at a sixth-grade level. Student is engaged in volunteer work through a church group. Student is able to use public transportation to travel in the community.

NEEDS: To learn more about social work and recreational activities in nursing homes. To develop better oral and written communication skills.

GOAL: To participate in service-learning programs to explore career options in working with the elderly persons and to develop social skills.

OBJECTIVES:

- To develop a profile of personal strengths and challenges for career planning.
- To meet with the counselor to explore service-learning opportunities in the community.
- To decide on a service-learning option that best meets my personal and vocational goals.

Project SUCCESS sponsored by the Department of Community and Recreation Services in Fairfax, VA (see: www.fairfaxcounty.gov/rec/projectsuccess.htm) is a nationally recognized model for inclusive service learning. It is designed for middle and high school students with and without disabilities. This program allows students of all ability levels the opportunity to become vested in the community while cultivating relationships with peers. Through this inclusive program, students with and without disabilities are empowered to become resourceful citizens. They learn to appreciate diversity and respect each other's unique capabilities. The website lists various services that the students have performed since the program's inception in 1998; for example, cooking meals at homeless shelters, making emergency bags for children in foster care, and planting community gardens, to name a few.

There are many potential benefits of service learning for students with disabilities. Service learning enables students with disabilities to practice important life skills and generalize learning. Serving in the community creates authentic situations for more natural peer relationships to develop. Perhaps most important, service learning provides students with disabilities an opportunity to give back to the community and to be a contributing member of society (Shoultz, Miller, & Ness, 2001).

Service Learning for Students with Social, Emotional, and Behavioral Impairments

Students exhibiting social, emotional, and behavioral problems typically do not respond to the traditional school curriculum and present challenges to teachers who are concerned about their academic progress. Instead of punishment, failure, or grade retention, more emphasis should be placed on meeting these students' needs for affiliation, accomplishment, and power (Glasser, 1985, 1998; Maslow, 1962/1999). As far back as 1983, Nicolaou and Brendtro recommended service learning as a curriculum of caring for students with social, emotional, and behavioral impairments. Service learning provides an authentic and multifaceted context for social, emotional, behavioral, and academic learning (Cairn & Cairn, 1999; Education Commission of the States, 2003; Yoder et al., 1996) and provides an opportunity to meet students' needs for affiliation, accomplishment, and power.

Despite the potential benefits of service learning for students with social, emotional, and behavioral impairments, they are often the recipients of service but seldom involved as service providers. Muscott (2001a) offered several reasons why students with social, emotional and behavioral impairments are rarely engaged as providers of service to others. First of all, the field of education has historically focused programming on the disability itself, emphasizing the remediation of the students' weaknesses rather than the enhancement of each student's strengths. Sometimes there is a pessimistic view that children and adolescents with social, emotional, and behavioral impairments have little, if anything, positive to offer others. A pragmatic concern is that students with these disabilities lack the requisite skills. Another concern is that students with social, emotional, and behavioral impairments lack the motivation and desire to perform acts of generosity for others.

Toward the end of the 20th century, service learning started to be recognized as a promising practice for students manifesting social, emotional, and behavioral problems (Frey, 2001, 2003; Muscott, 2001b, 2001c; Muscott & Talis O'Brien, 1999; Rockwell, 2001). Service learning is a strength-based practice (Frey, 1999). As such, service learning focuses thinking on students' strengths, leading to interventions based on those strengths. Peterson and Seligman (2004) recommended service learning as a deliberate intervention to promote positive social, emotional, and behavioral outcomes. Students who feel isolated, incompetent, and powerless in traditional classroom settings find they can learn and contribute in meaningful ways through service (Bullock & Fitzsimons-Lovett, 1997; Fitzsimons-Lovett, 1997; Ioele & Dolan, 1993).

For example, as an alternative to conducting groups focused on anger management, service-learning opportunities could be arranged to teach empathy, social skills, as well as emotional and behavioral regulation while addressing academic goals at the same time. Elias described just such an alternative to an anger management program (see Elias, Zins, Graczyk, & Weissberg, 2003). Virtually the same activities that were addressed in an anger management group, which the students resisted, were taught in the context of a Newspaper Club— listening, interacting with others, negotiating calmly, problem solving, in which the children participated enthusiastically. The students served the school and community by keeping them informed of current events through their newspaper. It is easy to see the potential ties to the academic curriculum in terms of writing skills, social studies, and math.

Billig (2000, 2002, 2004) revealed growing support for the social, emotional, and behavioral benefits of service learning. In fact, those benefits are the most consistently documented outcomes of service-learning experiences (Eyler & Giles, 1999). A statewide program evaluation in Texas documented the benefits of service learning for adjudicated youth in alternative school settings (Sneller, Billig, Palm, Webster, & Scoili, 2006). When service learning was substituted for punitive "community service" for these disenfranchised students, there were measurable gains in school and civic engagement. In addition, the community began to see these students in a more positive way. Across the state, different types of service projects were implemented at different locations, which suggest that the nature of the service was not the critical variable accounting for the changes, but rather, the process of serving itself. At this time, there is sufficient reason to be optimistic that service learning holds promise as an effective intervention for students with social, emotional, and behavioral impairments (Brigman & Molina, 1999; Kraft & Wheeler, 2003; Muscott, 2000).

Accommodations for Students with Social, Emotional, and Behavioral Impairments

There are, however, distinct challenges in implementing service-learning projects for students with social, emotional, and behavioral impairments. Because of their learning histories, these students may not have developed a sense of caring for others. They may see caring for others as a weakness or search for self-esteem by manipulating rather than serving others. Their limited social skills or impulsivity also may pose difficulties in cooperative group activities. For students with social, emotional, and behavioral impairments, Muscott (2001a, 2001b, 2001c) and Rockwell (2001) recommended designing service-learning projects that are highly structured with careful attention to group dynamics and individual learning needs. These students will need direct instruction in empathy and caring, explicitly drawing their attention to the needs of others. Service-learning project goals and objectives should be closely tied to the social, emotional, and behavioral goals and objectives listed on the student's IEP. Service learning may help integrate students in less restrictive school environments.

Project "Clean Sweep"

Consider the following example[1]: Service learning was employed as an intervention for eight sixth-grade middle school students at risk for academic failure due to personal and social adjustment difficulties. Teachers and administrators labeled the students as "behavior problems," and data showed that this group of students averaged three discipline referrals per week to the principal's office. Because of these referrals, instructional time was reduced dramatically.

In November, a service-learning program was initiated with all sixth-grade students in which students focused their attention on various school good deed projects to benefit the school, including playground clean-up, recycling bottles and cans, and decorating bulletin boards. These "good deeds" were ideas generated by students to improve school appearance, to be a part of the academic curriculum, and not considered as a punishment for inappropriate behavior. The school psychologist, counselor, and teachers collaborated to integrate academic lessons with the projects. In math class, for example, the students calculated the cost of clean-up activities and bottle recycling. Writing assignments included research papers on environmental issues and the importance of recycling. The eight "behavior problem" students were given the responsibility as leaders for collaborative teams of students on the service-learning projects. These students also took the lead in planning holiday decorations for the main office. After three months' time, the students reduced the number of discipline referrals to a total

---

[1] The authors gratefully acknowledge Rene Puopolo, graduate student at the University of Massachusetts Boston, for sharing this service-learning project.

of three! For the entire class, attendance increased, tardiness decreased, and the students reported that they liked school much better.

By participating in this service-learning project, these so-labeled behavior problem students became much more motivated toward school and felt more involved in the life of the school in a meaningful way. This project certainly can be said to have given these students a "purpose" for school. Also evident is the connection of academics with real-life skills and situations. This service-learning project is a wonderful illustration of simultaneously addressing specific emotional and social needs of students while teaching academic skills. This service-learning project is an authentic one that conveys a sense of purpose in helping with a real need in the school community. This is an especially important aspect of this project because the students involved in service learning were often not trusted with responsibility. Rather than focusing on the students' personal and social deficits, service learning involved them in a task with many dimensions that it became easy to find ways to capitalize on their strengths.

Helping with Middle School Transitions

Another example of a service-learning project that school psychologists or counselors could employ might be to enlist students with social and emotional difficulties to assist with an orientation program to welcome students transitioning from the elementary to middle school. Those students would plan the entire orientation, including an explanation of the school's core values of respect, responsibility, caring, trust, and family, and a demonstration of the expected behaviors. Students could design posters and perform skits to convey messages about positive school climate to incoming students. Students also might develop a handbook for new students. This activity would reinforce the codes of conduct for students who experience difficulty following school rules. The project can simultaneously address the specific needs of the students in terms of social interaction and emotional regulation while teaching the school's core values. Academic goals could be addressed through the various components of the service project. Concrete applications of academic skills can help students see the relevance of their classroom work in real life. Writing skills could be addressed through poster making and preparing a handbook. For math assignments, students could calculate the cost of the project or collect and analyze data about the orientation program's effectiveness. Such an orientation program is an authentic task that can convey a sense of purpose in helping with a real need in the school community. Rather than focusing on the children's social and emotional deficits, this type of service project involves students in a task with so many dimensions that it is easy to find ways to accommodate for students with special needs and capitalize on their strengths. Students get a deeper sense of the purpose of school values when they themselves experience those core values through their work. The following are prompts for student reflection about their experiences:

1. Describe the most caring thing you have ever done. Describe how you felt before and after.
2. What is the most important thing about this project that you have discovered so far? Why is this important to you?
3. Do members of your school community show you they care about you? If so, explain how. If not, explain why you feel this way.
4. How do you feel about your contributions to the orientation project? Do you feel good about accomplishing this? Explain why or why not.
5. Evaluate your performance so far in this project. What have you done really well? What do you think you could have done better?
6. Describe your feelings about the orientation project so far. Is it worthwhile? Why or why not? What do you like most about it? What do you wish could be different?
7. Is it important to serve your community? Why or why not?
8. Consider your work on the orientation project so far. How have you used math, reading, and writing skills to helping new students learn about your school?

Service-Learning Alternatives

The documented benefits of service learning found with general education students support an optimistic view that the same benefits will accrue to students with social, emotional, and behavioral impairments. Placing these students in special education and continuing to teach them in traditional ways has not been effective. Service learning is an ideal alternative for students with social, emotional, and behavioral impairments to get involved in their community, demonstrate their knowledge in practical situations, and experience a sense of accomplishment and pride.

References

Beirne-Smith, M., Ittenbach, R.F., & Patton, J. (1998). *Mental Retardation*, 5th ed., Columbus, OH: Merrill.

Berman, S. (1999). *Service-learning for the multiple intelligences classroom.* Arlington Heights, IL: Skylight Training and Publishing.

Billig, S.H. (2000). Research on K-12 school-based service-learning: The evidence builds. *Phi Delta Kappan, 81,* 658–664.

Billig, S.H. (2002). Support for K-12 service-learning practice. A brief review of the research. *Educational Horizons, 80,* 184–189.

Billig, S.H. (2004). Heads, hearts, and hands: The research on K-12 service-learning. In J. Kielsmeier, M. Neal, & M. McKinnon (Eds.), *Growing to greatness: The state of service-learning project* (pp. 12–25). St. Paul, MN: National Youth Leadership Council.

Brigman, G., & Molina, B. (1999). Developing social interest and enhancing school success skills: A service-learning approach. *Journal of Individual Psychology, 55,* 342–354.

Brill, C.R. (1994). The effects of participation in service-learning on adolescents with disabilities. *Journal of Adolescence, 17,* 369–380.

Bullock, L.M., & Fitzsimons-Lovett, A. (1997). Meeting the needs of children and youth with challenging behaviors. *Reaching Today's Youth: The Circle of Caring Journal, 2,* 50–56.

Burns, M., Storey, K., & Certo, N.J. (1999). Effect of service-learning on attitudes towards students with severe disabilities. *Education and Training in Mental Retardation and Developmental Disabilities, 34,* 58–65.

Cairn, R., & Cairn, S. (1999). Service-learning makes the grade. *Educational Leadership, 56*(6), 66–68.

Education Commission of the States. (2003). *Making the case for social and emotional learning and service-learning.* Denver, CO: Author.

Elias, M.J., Zins, J.E., Graczyk, P.A., & Weissberg, R.P. (2003). Implementation, sustainability, and scaling up of social–emotional and academic innovations in public schools. *School Psychology Review, 12,* 303–319.

Eyler, J., & Giles, D.E. (1999). *Where's the learning in service-learning?* Hoboken, NJ: John Wiley and Sons.

Fitzsimons-Lovett, A. (1997). Enhancing self-respect: A challenge for teachers of students with emotional/behavioral disorders. In L.M. Bullock & R.A. Gable (Eds.), *Second CCBD Mini-library series on emotional/behavioral disorders: Successful interventions for the 21st century.* Reston: VA: Council for Children with Behavioral Disorders.

Frey, L.M. (1999, Summer). Service-learning as a strength-based intervention. *Reclaiming children and youth, 8*(2), 98–101.

Frey, L.M. (2001, Spring). Integrating classroom academics with community-based learning; It's a win-win for all! *Beyond Behavior, 10*(3), 22–29.

Frey, L.M. (2003). Abundant beautification: An effective service-learning project for students with emotional or behavioral disorders. *Teaching Exceptional Children, 35*(5), 66–75.

Gardner, H. (1983). *Frames of mind: The theory of multiple intelligences.* New York: Basic Books.

Gardner, H. (2000). *Intelligence reframed: Multiple intelligences for the 21st century.* New York: Basic Books.

Gent, P.J., & Gurecka, L.E. (2001). Service-learning: A disservice to people with disabilities. *Michigan Journal of Community Service-Learning, 8,* 36–43.

Gent, P.J., & Gurecka, L.E. (2002). Service-learning: A creative strategy for inclusive classrooms. *Research and practice for persons with severe disabilities, 23,* 261–271.

Glasser, W. (1985). *Control theory in the classroom.* New York: Perennial Library.

Glasser, W. (1998). *Choice theory.* New York: Perennial Library.

Hampshire Educational Collaborative. (2003). *Inclusive service-learning: A training guide for K-12 teachers.* (National Service-Learning Clearinghouse Document No. 450/GC/HAM/2003).

Institute for Community Integration. (1999). *Yes I can: A social inclusion curriculum for students with and without disabilities.* (National Service-Learning Clearinghouse Document No. 450/G/ICI/1999)

Ioele, M.D., & Dolan, A.L. (1993). Teaching courage: Service-learning at the Pathway School. *Journal of Emotional and Behavioral Problems, 1,* 20–23.

Jennings, M. (2001). Two very special service-learning projects. *Phi Delta Kappan, 82,* 474–475.

Kleinert, H., McGregor, V., Durbin, M., Blandford, T., Jones, K., Owens, J., et al. (2004). Service-learning opportunities that include students with moderate and severe disabilities. *Teaching Exceptional Children, 27*(2), 28–34.

Klopp, C., Toole, P., & Toole, J. (2001). *Pondering learning: Connecting multiple intelligences and service-learning.* Clemson, SC: National Dropout Prevention Center.

Kluth, P. (2000). Community-referenced learning and the inclusive classroom. *Remedial & Special Education, 21*, 19–26.

Kraft, N., & Wheeler, J. (2003). Service-learning and resilience in disaffected youth: A research study. In S.H. Billig & J. Eyler (Eds.), *Deconstructing service-learning: Research exploring context, participation, and impacts* (pp. 213–238). Greenwich, CT: Information Age Publishing.

Maryland Student Service Alliance. (1993). *Service-learning special education guide.* Maryland State Department of Education: Author. Available at http://www.marylandpublicschools.org/MSDE.

Maslow, A. (1962/1999). *Toward a psychology of being*, 3rd ed. New York: John Wiley and Sons.

Morales, W. (1999). *Project Success: Service-learning and students with disabilities.* (National Service-Learning Clearinghouse Document No. 450/B/MOR/1999).

Muscott, H.S. (2000). A review and analysis of service-learning programs involving students with behavioral disorders. *Education and Treatment of Children, 23*, 346–368.

Muscott, H.S. (2001a, Spring). An introduction to service-learning for students with emotional and behavioral disorders: Answers to frequently asked questions. *Beyond Behavior, 10*(3), 8–15.

Muscott, H.S. (2001b, Spring). Fostering learning, fun, and friendship among students with emotional disorders and their peers: The SO (service-learning) prepared for citizenship program. *Beyond Behavior, 10*(3), 36–47.

Muscott, H.S. (2001c, Summer). Service-learning and character education as "antidotes" for children with egos that cannot perform. *Reclaiming Children and Youth, 10*(2), 91–99.

Muscott, H.S., & Talis O'Brien, S. (1999). Teaching character education to students with behavioral and learning disabilities through mentoring relationships. *Education and Treatment of Children, 22*, 373–390.

National Service Inclusion Project [NSIP]. (n.d.). *Integrating service-learning in individual educational plans for primary school students with disabilities.* Retrieved March 3, 2006, from http://www.nationalserviceresources.org/resources/tta/university_mass.php.

National Service Inclusion Project [NSIP]. (2003, December 18). *Application of universal curriculum design to service-learning projects* [Teleconference]. Boston: Author

National Service-Learning Clearinghouse. Retrieved March 3, 2006, from http://www.servicelearning.org.

Neal, M., & Holland, B. (2005). Symbiosis: When service-learning meets the work of Howard Gardner. In National Youth Leadership Council, *Growing to Greatness 2005* (pp. 29–33). St. Paul, MN: Author.

Nicolaou, A., & Brendtro, L.K. (1983). Curriculum for caring: Service-learning for behaviorally disordered students. In R.B. Rutherford, Jr. (Ed.), *Monograph in behavioral disorders: severe behavior disorders of children and youth* (Vol. 6, pp. 108–114). Reston, VA: Council for Children with Behavior Disorders.

Peterson, C., & Seligman, M.E.P. (2004). *Character strengths and virtues: A handbook and classification.* New York: Oxford University Press and Washington, DC: American Psychological Association.

Rockwell, S. (2001, Spring). Service-learning: Barriers, benefits, and models of excellence. *Beyond Behavior, 10*(3), 16–21.

Service-Learning Network. (Winter, 2002). *Service-learning and special education, 9*(2). Los Angeles, CA: Constitutional Rights Foundation. Retrieved September 9, 2005, from http://www/crf-usa.org/network/net9_2.htm.

Shoultz, B., Miller, E.E., & Ness, J. (2001). Volunteerism by persons with developmental disabilities [Special Issue]. *Impact, 14*(2).

Sneller, S., Billig, S., Palm, D., Webster, M.A., Scoili, D. (2006, March). *Proof: Service-learning benefits disenfranchised students.* Paper presented at the annual meeting of the National Youth Leadership Council, Philadelphia, PA.

Students in Service to America. Retrieved March 3, 2006, from http://www.studentsinservicetoamerica.org.

Yoder, D., Retish, E., & Wade, R. (1996). Service-learning: Meeting student and community needs. *Teaching Exceptional Children, 28*(4), 14–18.

8
Reducing Risk-Taking Behaviors

Service Learning to Reduce Health Risk Taking

By all accounts, psychological distress is rampant in schools today, and for many students, significantly interferes with their academic achievement (Columbia University, 2003). The distress often takes the form of depression and anxiety, now being considered as two sides of the same coin, which leads to disengagement from the community and substance abuse. Substance abuse refers to any mood-altering drug that is taken for nonmedical reasons, including alcohol, tobacco, marijuana, and prescription drugs, among others. Many physical changes occur as a result of alcohol, tobacco, or drug abuse and these changes can make concentration and learning in school more difficult (US Department of Education, 2006). Moreover, illnesses due to a weakened immune systems, as well as dependency and withdrawal symptoms, lead to increased absences from school.

In Boston (Boston Public Health Commission [BPHC], 2003), two out of five high school seniors reported using alcohol within the last month and one in five reported binge drinking. Statistics provided by Mothers against Drunk Driving (MADD, 2004) indicated that motor vehicle accidents are the leading cause of death among adolescents, and more than one-third of all traffic fatalities involving 15- to 20-year-olds are alcohol-related. In addition, according to the results of a statewide survey in Massachusetts (BPHC, 2003), adolescents who reported alcohol use were twice as likely to have attempted suicide in the past year as compared with their nondrinking peers. After motor vehicle accidents and homicide, suicide is the third leading cause of death for adolescents (US Department of Health and Human Services, 2003).

Schools typically respond to substance abuse by enforcing laws and working with the community to curtail access. Nonclinical depression is usually medicalized and treated with drugs, which students often abuse. Both approaches are strategies to control the consequences of student disengagement rather than encouraging student engagement in school and community.

Fortunately, programs serving youth at risk for mental and physical health problems have been slowly shifting from a stigmatizing, pathological perspective toward prevention and positive development. In fact, the evidence shows that programs work best when they target risk and protective factors rather than specific problem behaviors (Greenberg, Domitrovich, & Bumbarger, 2001; Schinke, Brounstein, & Gardner, 2002). Engaging students in learning contexts, such as meaningful service learning, is a promising strategy for prevention and intervention. Seligman (2005) noted that one consistent finding in the research literature is that engagement is correlated with lower risk of substance abuse and depression. He suggested that engagement might be a necessary condition for positive health and development. Service learning is just such a tool for engagement. It has been shown to contribute to student resiliency in making positive alternative choices to substance abuse, and for those students at risk for depression, in finding purpose through activities beyond themselves.

How does service learning promote engagement and prevent health-risk behaviors? Service learning strengthens academic learning for students by getting them involved in experiencing and understanding the relationship of what they study in class to issues outside of themselves. Service learning may contribute to adolescent well-being by fostering identity development as well as dispositions that make resistance to peer pressure more likely. Service learning can convey a sense of responsibility that forces adolescents to reflect upon their own perspectives and privileges. If students are engaged in defining and solving problems, they are less likely to be overwhelmed by them. Student engagement in socially valued tasks is a critical protective factor in preventing social problems.

Protecting You, Protecting Me (see www.pypm.org) is a nationally recognized alcohol use prevention curriculum for grades one to five. Trained high school students help elementary school children, parents, and community leaders learn about the dangers of underage alcohol use. As influential role models, adolescents can have a positive impact on young children's knowledge and attitudes about substance abuse. As leaders, adolescents become responsible for positive change in their communities. As teachers, adolescents "listen to their own advice" and start to make better choices. The program is based on principles for effective social–emotional learning and meets the requirements of the No Child Left Behind (NCLB) Act and the Safe and Drug Free Schools and Communities (SDFSC) Act. The US Department of Health and Human Services, Substance Abuse and Mental Health Services Administration (SAMHSA) recognizes *Protecting You, Protecting Me* as a model program. The program has been adapted for Native American communities and a Spanish version of the curriculum is also available.

Project Venture is a prevention program that includes a service-learning component adapted for Native American students at risk for substance abuse. The program has been shown significant reductions in delaying the onset of alcohol use and reducing current alcohol, tobacco, and other drug use (see http://niylp.org/programs/project_venture and http://www.modelprograms.samhsa.gov).

Thompson, Lyman, Childers, and Taylor (2002) involved adolescents in an interactive way with their communities to address the consequences of drug abuse. Students helped the organization, MADD, gather data about Driving while Intoxicated (DWI) court cases. Students attended judicial proceedings involving DWI and summarized the facts of the case for MADD to use in their safe driving campaigns. The students also reflected on the consequences of DWI offenses. This service-learning experience placed the students in close proximity to the problem and consequences of drunk driving while fulfilling an authentic need to collect data for state legislators regarding the effectiveness of current DWI laws.

Project Ignition (see http://www.sfprojectignition.com) incorporates service learning to address the issue of teen driver safety for students in grades 9 through 12. Students arrange community-based events to raise awareness about dangerous driving habits and to promote safe driving among their peers and within the community at large.

School is an important arena for social and emotional as well as academic development. As such, it is a desirable setting to address mental health and substance abuse issues. School psychologists and counselors can address problems of alcohol, tobacco, and other drug abuse as well as the underlying depression through myriad service-learning projects that can also connect to the academic curriculum. If students are attached to school, they are less likely to violate the standards of that institution. The active ingredient for positive development is engagement, and service learning is an approach found to be effective in dealing with challenging mental health and substance abuse issues.

Service Learning to Reduce Sexual Risk Taking

Teen pregnancy and school failure top the list of important adolescent social problems because of their costly consequences to the young people themselves and to society as a whole. Adolescent sexual behavior brings, besides pregnancy, a significant risk of contracting HIV. A multitude of programs have targeted adolescent sexual risk taking to reduce unintended pregnancy and sexually transmitted diseases. Instead of efforts to address risk behaviors individually, Scales (1990) argued in favor of holistic efforts to improve the cognitive, behavioral, and social competencies of youth. Kirby's review (2002) confirmed that even though many programs report some positive effects for specific outcomes (e.g., greater knowledge), only programs that address broad-based positive youth development rather than individual problem behaviors have actually delayed the initiation of sex and reduced unprotected sex among adolescents. Service learning is just such a vehicle to promote positive development.

Service learning has a stronger evidence of reducing teen pregnancy rates while adolescents are in the program than does any other type of intervention (Hahn, Leavitt, & Aaron, 1994; Johns, Moncloa, & Gong, 2000; Kirby & Coyle, 1997; Melchior, 1999; O'Donnell et al., 1999). However, it is not clear why service learning is effective in preventing unintended pregnancy. Service-learning programs are multifaceted and there are many possible reasons for an increase in the motivation to avoid pregnancy. In service-learning programs, adolescents develop caring relationships with others and gain a greater sense of interpersonal competence. When adolescents realize that they are able to make a difference in the community through their service, they may see more options for themselves in the future. Moreover, because community service is time-intensive, there is less opportunity for youths to engage in sexual risk behaviors.

On the basis of his review, Kirby (2002) suggested that traditional sex education and service learning were complementary approaches that, taken together, may prove most effective. Traditional sex education focuses on the sexual antecedents of risk-taking behavior (such as beliefs, attitudes, norms), while service learning focuses on the nonsexual antecedents (such as connections to adults and hope for the future). Denner, Coyle, Robin, and Banspach, (2005) emphasized the importance of student reflection to create positive service-learning experiences.

Reducing adolescent sexual risk behavior is a primary goal of the Teen Outreach Program (TOP). In 1978 Brenda Hostetler, director of pregnancy prevention programs in St. Louis, MO, Public Schools, developed the program. The TOP is a flexible and comprehensive youth development program that focuses on self-image, life skills, and setting achievable goals. It consists of a classroom component and a community service experience, both of which are considered to be key elements in the success of the TOP. In the classroom, students develop communication and problem-solving skills and address issues such as interpersonal relationships, peer pressure, family problems, and life options. The service component enhances students' sense of self-worth as they come to see themselves as contributing members of the community—helpers rather than help seekers. In addition, the service work provides students with the opportunity for vocational exploration and for developing job skills.

The TOP is a national program that is currently being implemented in schools and agencies across the United States. It is one the most carefully evaluated and successful pregnancy prevention programs for adolescents. In addition to lowering pregnancy rates, students who participated in the TOP also increase their academic achievement (Allen, Kuperminc, Philliber, & Herr, 1994; Allen, Philliber, Herring, & Kuperminc, 1997; Allen, Philliber, & Hoggson, 1990; Kirby, 2001; Miller, Card, Paikoff, & Peterson, 1992). The effectiveness of the TOP in ameliorating these two very different problems suggests that high-risk behaviors may share a common cause.

Notable about the research findings of Allen et al. is that the effectiveness of the TOP is not dependent on the integrity with which the program is implemented, suggesting that the service itself is the critical component. Furthermore, the service does not have to be explicitly designed to point out the difficulties of early parenthood. It is the involvement in contributory service that is the key element. Allen and Philliber (2001) reported that the TOP is most effective as a prevention program for adolescents who were most at risk for problematic behavior. The program had the greatest impact in reducing future pregnancies among those who had already given birth and were at highest risk for another pregnancy.

The TOP supports positive youth development by providing service-learning opportunities to enhance self-esteem and self-confidence in an authentic context that allows students to remain engaged with school and the community (Allen et al., 1994). One striking feature of the TOP is that it does not explicitly focus on the sexual risk-taking behavior it seeks to prevent, but rather seeks to foster adolescents' social and emotional adjustment. A service-learning preventive approach might be more politically acceptable in some communities where programs specifically focusing on sex education and pregnancy prevention may not be feasible.

Other programs that address sexual risk-taking behavior by taking an empowerment perspective to bolster self-esteem and to change adolescents' worldviews include All 4 You (Denner et al., 2005), Cooperative Extension Human Resource Program (Johns et al., 2000), Reach for Health (O'Donnell et al., 1999), and Quantum Opportunities Program (Hahn et al., 1994). Service learning is a critical component of each of those programs and by itself is a promising approach to reduce sexual risk behavior and improve school achievement.

References

Allen, J.P., Kuperminc, G.P., Philliber, S., & Herre, K. (1994). Programmatic prevention of adolescent problem behaviors: The role of autonomy, relatedness and volunteer service in the Teen Outreach Program. *American Journal of Community Psychology*, 22, 617–638.

Allen, J.P., & Philliber, S. (2001). Who benefits most from a broadly targeted prevention program? Differential efficacy across populations in the Teen Outreach Program. *Journal of Community Psychology*, 29, 637–655.

Allen, J.P., Philliber, S., Herring, S., & Kuperminc, G.P. (1997). Preventing teen pregnancy and academic failure: Experimental evaluation of a developmentally based approach. *Child Development*, 64, 729–742.

Allen, J.P., Philliber, S., & Hoggson, N. (1990). School-based prevention of teen-age pregnancy and school dropout: Process evaluation of the national replication of the Teen Outreach Program. *American Journal of Community Psychology*, 18, 505–524.

Boston Public Health Commission. (2003). *The health of Boston*. Retrieved April 3, 2006, from http://www.bphc.org/news/report.asp?id=160.

Columbia University. (2003, September). *Catch them before they fall: How to implement mental health screening programs for youth as recommended by the President's New Freedom Commission on Mental Health*. Retrieved April 3, 2006, from http://www.ecs.org/html/issue.asp?issueid=213.

Denner, J., Coyle, K., Robin, L., & Banspach, S. (2005). Integrating service-learning into a curriculum to reduce health risks at alternative high schools. *Journal of School Health*, 75(5), 151–156.

Greenberg, M.T., Domitrovich, C., & Bumbarger, B. (2001). The prevention of mental disorders in school-age children: Current state of the field. *Prevention & Treatment*, 4. Retrieved April 5, 2006, from http://journals.apa.org/prevention/.

Hahn, A., Leavitt, T., & Aaron, P. (1994). *Evaluation of the Quantum Opportunities Program (QOP). Did the program work? A report on the post-secondary outcomes and cost-effectiveness of the QOP program.* (ERIC Document Reproduction Service No. ED 385 621).

Johns, M.J., Moncloa, F., & Gong, E.J. (2000). Teen pregnancy prevention programs: Linking research and practice. *Journal of Extension, 38*(4). [Online]. Retrieved March 17, 2006, from http://www.joe.org/joe/2000august/a1.html.

Kirby, D. (2001). *Emerging answers: Research findings on programs to reduce teen pregnancy.* Washington, DC: National Campaign to Prevent Teen Pregnancy. Retrieved March 17, 2006, from http://www.teenpregnancy.org/resources/data/pdf/emeranswsum.pdf.

Kirby, D. (2002). Effective approaches to reducing adolescent unprotected sex, pregnancy, and childbearing. *Journal of Sex Research, 39,* 51–57.

Kirby, D., & Coyle, K. (1997). School-based programs to reduce sexual risk taking behavior. *Children and Youth Services Review, 19,* 415–436.

Melchior, A. (1999, July). *Summary report: National evaluation of Learn and Serve America and community-based programs.* Waltham, MA: Center for Human Resources, Brandeis University. Retrieved March 17, 2006, from http://www.learnandserve.gov/pdf/lsa_evaluation.pdf.

Miller, B., Card, J.J., Paikoff, R.L., & Peterson, J.L. (Eds.). (1992). *Preventing adolescent pregnancy: Model program and evaluations.* Newbury Park, CA: Sage Publications.

Mothers against Drunk Driving. (2004). *Fatalities and alcohol-related fatalities among 15–20 year olds.* Retrieved April 3, 2006, from http://www.madd.org/stats/9659.

O'Donnell, L., Stueve, A., San Doval, A., Duran, R., Haber, D., Atnafou, R., et al. (1999). The effectiveness of Reach for Health community youth service program in reducing early and unprotected sex among urban middle school students. *American Journal of Public Health, 89,* 176–181.

Scales, R. (1990). Developing capable young people: An alternative strategy for prevention programs. *Journal of Early Adolescence, 10,* 420–438.

Schinke, S., Brounstein, P., & Gardner, S. (2002). *Science-based prevention programs.* Rockville, MD: Department of Health and Human Services, Center for Substance Abuse Prevention. Retrieved April 5, 2006, from http://modelprograms.samhsa.gov/pdfs/2001Annual.pdf.

Seligman, M.E.P. (2005, April). *Positive psychology at school.* Keynote address delivered at the annual meeting of the National Association of School Psychologists. Atlanta, GA.

Thompson, G.D., Lyman, S., Childers, K., and Taylor, P. (2002). Strategy for alcohol abuse education: A service-learning model within a course curriculum. *American Journal of Health Education, 23,* 88–93.

US Department of Education. (2006). *Linking violence and substance abuse prevention to academic success.* Washington, DC: Author. Retrieved April 5, 2006, from http://www.ed.gov/admins/lead/safety/training/linking/academic_pg5.html.

US Department of Health and Human Services. (2003). *Child Health USA.* Washington, DC: Author. Retrieved April 5, 2006, from http://www.mchb.hrsa.gov/chusa03/pages/status_adolescents.htm.

9
Preventing School Failure

Preventing Dropout

A report recently released by the Coalition for Community Schools (Melaville, Berg, & Blank, 2006) cites research indicating that 40% to 60% of *all* students— urban, suburban, and rural—are chronically disengaged from school. The report also highlighted disengagement as a key factor in the dropout rate: 47% of the dropouts who were surveyed left school because their classes were not interesting. It appears that alienation and disaffection among students occurs within the climate of disengagement prevalent in many schools and communities. A special issue of the *Journal of School Health* (Blum & Libbey, 2004) examined how disengagement from school and community decreases students' prospects for academic success and leads to school dropouts.

Nationally, 68% of all students entering grade-nine graduate in four years. Among school dropouts are a disproportionately high number of poor and minority students. While the graduation rate for White students is approximately 75%, only about 50% of Black, Latino, and Native American students earn regular high school diplomas; graduation rates are even lower for minority males (Harvard Civil Rights Project, 2005; Orfield, 2004). Students from low-income families drop out of school at double the rate of that from middle-income and six times of that from upper-income families (US Department of Education, 2004).

Withdrawing from school is a process of academic or social disengagement over time, the final event in a sequence that might have begun years before (Wilczenski, 1994). School dropout is not simply a function of low attendance, learning disabilities, poor grades, unsatisfactory peer relationships, substance abuse, and delinquency. Although all these factors may contribute, the underlying cause of dropout can be traced to a process of disengagement that can begin in elementary school. Students who disengage from school also receive teacher responses that may further undermine motivation.

There is mounting evidence that school engagement is an important developmental asset for children and adolescents (Search Institute, 1997). Engagement is the sense of attachment that students feel when they perceive that adults care about them as individuals and as learners. Payne (2005) suggested that these relationships are key motivators for students from poverty. Service learning helps schools create these relationships. Dr. Robert Blum (2005) of Johns Hopkins University provided a wonderful example of meaningful community engagement for youth who are at risk for dropout: A school in Spanish Harlem in New York City enlisted students who were failing academically to be teachers of English as a second language. They offered a night course to taxi drivers. The adults learned English and the students bolstered their self-esteem by learning that they had something important to contribute to their community. Engagement in learning is closely linked to student achievement and reduced dropout rates (Bartko, 1999; Blank, 1997; Duckenfield & Drew, 2006; Meyer, 2004; Woods, 1995).

Service to others may function as a "gateway" asset enabling other developmental assets to contribute to positive outcomes (Scales & Rochlkepartain, 2004). Service learning is a powerful way to demonstrate to students that they are cared for and to give students something to care about. The National Dropout Prevention Center (2004) lists service learning as an effective strategy for dropout prevention across K-12 grade levels.

New research also suggests that engagement in service learning may be of particular benefit for disadvantaged students in closing the achievement gap between low- and high-income students. Service learning increases engagement and motivation among students at risk for school failure. There are data indicating that service learning contributes to equity of academic achievement for disadvantaged students (Scales & Rochlkepartain, 2005). Scales, Rochlkepartain, Neal, Kielsmeier, and Benson (2005) found that service of only one hour per week among low-income students was related to a significant reduction in the gap of achievement-related issues, such as attendance and homework, as compared to low-income students who did not participate in service. Meyer, Hofshire, and Billig (2004) proposed that engagement mediates the relationship between service learning and academic achievement.

When asked what schools need to do to engage students, the Coalition of Community Schools report indicated that 81% of dropouts called for more "real-world" learning experiences (Melaville et al., 2006). If educators are really serious about leaving no child behind, schools need to present academic content in a context that has meaning and relevance in students' everyday lives. By providing an authentic context for learning and by reinforcing students' sense of belonging to a community, service learning may help to increase the engagement and motivation of disadvantaged students at highest risk for school dropout.

Research has revealed several components of service learning that are likely to increase student engagement (Brewster & Fager, 2000), such as:

- Demonstrating ways that learning can be applied to the "real world."
- Helping students to feel that their schoolwork is significant, valuable, and worthy of effort.
- Allowing students to have some degree of control over learning.
- Setting challenging but achievable goals.
- Stimulating students' curiosity about the subject matter.
- Designing projects that allow students to share what they have learned with others.

Service learning is an effective means of meeting the goals of the No Child Left Behind (NCLB) Act of 2001, Title I (Improving the Academic Achievement of the Disadvantaged), by connecting academic learning with real-life situations (Billig & Brown, 2002; NCLB, 2001). The Dropout Prevention Act (Title I, Part H) supports service learning for school dropout prevention and re-entry and for ensuring that students have ongoing opportunities to reach their highest academic potential. The content of the service activity itself is not the critical variable, it is the process of serving that is most important in achieving positive outcomes.

"First Opportunity" at the Folwell Middle School in Minneapolis, Minnesota, is an early-intervention service-learning program designed for 11- to 15-year-old low-income students who are at risk for school dropout. It is a holistic approach that encompasses community service, mentoring, life skills training, and family outreach. One service-learning activity trains students as peer mediators who then teach other students conflict resolution skills. An increase in school attendance was documented for students participating in service-learning projects (See http://www.servicelearning.org/resources/online_documents/the_2001_no_child_left_behind_act/title_i_part_h_school_dropout_prevention_17k_pdf/.

Malcolm Shabazz City High School in Madison, Wisconsin, integrates service learning in all aspects of its curriculum for youth who are at risk for dropout. The "Stress Challenge" project addresses problem solving, communication, "smart" risk-taking, and respect for others. High school students learn to trust each other through cooperative activities such as rope climbing. They then serve as role models by involving younger children cooperative climbing gym activities. The Shabazz High School website describes other community/service-learning partnerships that have sparked excitement at the school (see http://www.madison.k12.wi.us/shabazz/sl/slintro.html).

The good news is that research confirms that service learning has a profound impact on student engagement by making learning relevant and meaningful. School engagement is an important developmental asset and protector factor in preventing school dropout. Service learning has research to support its usefulness in motivating students who are disengaged from school, and therefore, as an evidence-based strategy, school psychologists and counselors need to incorporate service learning in dropout prevention programs.

School-to-Work Transitions

In an address to the National Congress of Parents and Teachers in 1942, William Carr (1942) argued:

Many schools are like little islands set apart from the mainland of life by a deep moat of convention and tradition. Across this moat there is a drawbridge which is lowered at certain periods during the day in order that the part-time inhabitants may cross over to the island in the morning and back to the mainland at night. Why do these young people go out to the island? They go there to learn how to live on the mainland.

The quote highlights the challenges still faced by schools and communities today to make learning meaningful and useful. Students disengage from or drop out of school for several reasons: (1) dissatisfaction with the isolation of school from the real world; (2) lack of understanding of the relevance of academic skills; and (3) complaints of boredom and restlessness. One of the primary purposes of recent educational reform efforts is to enable all students to become productive, independent, caring adults who contribute to the welfare of their communities. Effective dropout retrieval and school-to-work transition programs are employing active learning as a strategy and service learning as a methodology (Carter, 2001).

Transitioning from the dependency of childhood to the full responsibilities of adulthood is problematic for many adolescents. Because the traditional school environment does not meet the needs of all students, especially those students who are disengaged, alternative strategies must be developed. Authentically engaging students in contributing to their communities through service learning is a credible response to the issues raised by this adolescent turmoil. Service learning provides students with tools for the transition to adulthood. The sense of responsibility, independence, and maturity that service learning conveys are the same characteristics that mark adulthood. Martin, Neal, Kielsmeier, and Crossley (2006) summarized the results of a national survey that indicated adults who participated in service learning during their school years were more likely than their peers to:

- be politically and socially connected to their communities;
- serve as role models for young adults;
- understand the importance of lifelong learning;
- attain a higher level of education; and
- engage in service.

Because service learning accommodates multiple intelligences (Gardner, 1983), it also can help students identify their strengths and weaknesses as well as possible career interests (Murry, 2001). Traditional school-to-work models link with the community by placing students at a job site to develop technical skills and work habits. Service learning deliberately links these work site activities to the school curriculum. When the two are yoked as work-based service learning, they bring a new vitality to the school curriculum whereby students gain work experience while contributing to their communities (Boyer, 1987; Dunlap, 1998). Communities benefit by a prepared workforce. Students benefit by:

- an enhanced academic curriculum,
- applying classroom learning,
- opportunities to explore or to confirm career goals,
- acquiring technical workplace skills,
- learning interpersonal workplace skills,
- developing personal work habits,
- a stronger resume, and
- an improved image of school within the community.

Often, students with disabilities have difficulty in meeting high school graduation requirements. There are mounting concerns about the relationship of their school experiences and postschool transition plans that address postsecondary education, employment, and living arrangements (Johnson, Sharpe, & Stodden, 2000). Special education teams constructing Individual Educational Plans (IEPs) must ensure that students with disabilities are provided with appropriate transition services (Hasazi, Furney, & DeStefano, 1999; Witte, 2002). Work-based service learning can help students with disabilities meet career-related learning IEP goals and objectives, such as:

- Personal management: Exhibit appropriate work ethics and behaviors.
- Problem solving: Apply systematic decision making.
- Communication: Give and receive information effectively.
- Teamwork: Work well with others to accomplish a task.
- Employability: Demonstrate requisite academic, technical, and organizational knowledge and job skills.
- Career development: Engage in appropriate transition planning for post-high schoolwork and life.

Dunlap (1998) provides a compendium of work-based service-learning activities and potential partners. For example, a student interested in a health- or education-related occupation might teach swimming, life saving, or CPR at a local YMCA/YWCA. Students interested in engineering or science-related occupations could assist an environmental agency with water or air quality testing. Construction skills can be honed by working with Habitat for Humanity. Those students with interests in the arts, media, or communication may work as a docent in a museum. In all cases, it is important to fully integrate the school-to-work program with the service-learning framework. Best practices for work-based service learning include the following:

- defined expectations,
- clear connections with the school curriculum,
- meaningful work,
- adequate supervision,
- developmentally appropriate activities,
- opportunities for reflection, and
- recognition of contributions.

Service learning and school-to-work both extend learning beyond the classroom into real-world contexts where broader problem-solving and decision-making skills are addressed. While service learning provides opportunities for students to participate in learning activities within their community to use their academic and vocational competencies, school-to-work helps students make tentative career choices and develop educational goals aimed at achieving vocational and personal satisfaction. The National Service-Learning Clearinghouse (n.d.)

compiled a bibliography of references pertaining to this topic for grades K-12 (www.servicelearning.org).

School psychologists and counselors know that education plays a major role in life success. Instead of the obsolete drawbridges to which Carr referred, service learning builds bridges uniting schools and communities that allow students to connect their actions to the "real" world outside of the classroom. The ultimate goal is to graduate youth from high school with a plan in place to get a job, to attend college, or to enroll in a trade or apprenticeship program. By providing opportunities for personal, social, career, and academic growth, work-based service learning can smoothen the transition from adolescence to successful employment and adulthood for all students.

References

Bartko, W.T. (1999). *Student engagement and development.* Ann Arbor, MI: University of Michigan.

Billig, S.H., & Brown, S. (2002). *Opportunities for service-learning in the No Child Left Behind Act of 2001.* Denver, CO: RMC Research Corporation. Retrieved March 3, 2005, from http://www.servicelearning.org.

Blank, W. (1997). Authentic instruction. In W.E. Blank & S. Harwell (Eds.), *Promising practices for connecting high school to the real world* (pp. 15–21). Tampa, FL: University of South Florida. (Eric Document Reproduction Service No. ED 407 586).

Blum, R.W. (2005). *School connectedness and meaningful student participation.* Retrieved April 11, 2006, from http://www.ed.gov/admins/lead/safety/training/connect/school_pg21.html.

Blum, R.W., & Libbey, H.P. (Eds.). (2004). Wingspread declaration on school connections [Special edition]. *Journal of School Health, 74*(7).

Boyer, E.L. (1987). Service: Linking school to life. *Community Education Journal, 15,* 7–9.

Brewster, C., & Fager, J. (2000). *Increasing student engagement and motivation: From time-on-task to homework.* Portland, OR: Northwest Regional Educational Laboratory. Retrieved April 11, 2006, from http://www.nwrel.org/request/oct00/textonly.html.

Carr, W.G. (1942). *Community life in a democracy.* Washington, DC: National Congress of Parents and Teachers.

Carter, K.G. (2001). *Hooking out-of-school youth through service-learning.* Columbia, SC: Department of Education.

Duckenfield, M., & Drew, S. (2006). Measure what matters and no child will be left behind. In *Growing to greatness: The state of service-learning project* (pp. 33–39). St. Paul, MN: National Youth Leadership Council.

Dunlap, N.C. (1998). *School to work to life: Linking service-learning and school-to-work.* Columbia, SC: Department of Education.

Gardner, H. (1983). *Frames of mind.* New York: Basic Books.

Harvard University. (2005). *Civil Rights Project.* Retrieved April 7, 2006, from http://www.civilrightsproject.harvard.edu/research/dropouts/dropouts05.php.

Hasazi, S.B., Furney, K.S., & DeStefano, L. (1999). Implementing the IDEA transition mandates. *Exceptional Children, 65,* 555–566.

Johnson, D.R., Sharpe, M., & Stodden, R. (2000). The transition to postsecondary education for students with disabilities. *IMPACT, 13*(1), 26–27. Minneapolis, MN: Institute on Community Integration, University of Minnesota.

Martin, S., Neal, M., Kielsmeier, J.C., & Crossley, A. (2006). *The impact of service-learning on transitions to adulthood. Growing to greatness: The state of service-learning project* (pp. 4–24). St. Paul, MN: National Youth Leadership Council.

Melaville, A., Berg, A.C., & Blank, M.J. (2006). *Community-based learning: Engaging students for success and citizenship.* Washington, DC: Coalition for Community Schools. Retrieved April 7, 2006, from http://www.communityschools.org.

Meyer, S.J. (2004). *Service-learning and student engagement.* Denver, CO: RMC Research Corporation.

Meyer, S.J., Hofshire, L., & Billig, S.H. (2004). *The impact of service-learning on MEAP: A large scale study of Michigan Learn & Serve Grantees.* Denver, CO: RMC Research Corporation.

Murry, F. (2001, Spring). Aerosol is not a gang art: Service-learning can become a living. *Beyond Behavior, 10*(3), 48–53.

National Dropout Prevention Center. (2004). *15 effective strategies for dropout prevention.* Clemson University, SC: Author. Retrieved April 7, 2006, from http://www.dropoutprevention.org/effstrat/effstrat.htm.

National Service-Learning Clearinghouse. (n.d.) *Career exploration and service-learning bibliography.* Scotts Valley, CA: Author. Retrieved June 29, 2006, from http://www.servicelearning.org/lib_svcs/bibs/he_bibs/career/.

Orfield, G. (2004). *Dropouts in America: Confronting the graduation rate crisis.* Retrieved April 6, 2006, from http://www.gse.harvard.edu/hepg/dropoutsinamerica.html.

Payne, R.K. (2005). *A framework for understanding poverty* (rev. ed.). Highlands, TX: aha! Process.

Scales, P.C., & Rochlkepartain, E.C. (2004). Service to others: A 'gateway' asset for school success and healthy development. In *Growing to greatness: The state of service-learning project* (pp. 26–32). St. Paul, MN: National Youth Leadership Council.

Scales, P.C., & Rochlkepartain, E.C. (2005). Can service-learning help reduce the achievement gap? In *Growing to greatness: The state of service-learning project* (pp. 10–22). St. Paul, MN: National Youth Leadership Council.

Scales, P.C., Rochlkepartain, E.C., Neal, M., Kielsmeier, J.C., & Benson, P.L. (2005). *The contribution of community service and service-learning to academic achievement among socio-economically disadvantaged students.* Minneapolis, MN: Search Institute.

Search Institute. (1997). *40 developmental assets.* Minneapolis, MN: Author.

US Department of Education. (2004). *The condition of education 2004.* Washington, DC: National Center for Education Statistics. Retrieved March 3, 2005, from http://www.nces.ed.gov.

Wilczenski, F.L. (1994). Impact of school participation and disengagement on first grade achievement. *Journal of Research in Education, 4*, 53–57.

Witte, R. (2002). Best practices in transition to post-secondary work. In A. Thomas & J. Grimes (Eds.), *Best practices in school psychology—IV* (pp. 1585–1597). Bethesda, MD: National Association of School Psychologists.

Woods, E.G. (1995). Reducing the dropout rate. In *School improvement research series (SIRS): Research you can use* (Close-Up No. 17). Portland, OR: Northwest Regional Educational Laboratory. Retrieved April 11, 2006, from http://www.nwrel.org/scpd/sirs/9/c017.html.

10
Fostering a Positive School Climate

Violence Prevention

Violence is a one of the greatest concerns of youth in this country (Horatio Alger Association, 2005). Homicide is the second leading cause of death among adolescents (US Department of Health and Human Services, 2003). Recent headlines about horrific shooting incidents in our nation's schools provide ample evidence of the problem of youth violence. But violence in schools is not just about murder, it is also about the many other acts of interpersonal and physical violence (harassment, bullying, physical aggression, child abuse, date rape) that are barriers to academic learning. The students who commit the most serious acts of violence feel disengaged from school and alienated from classmates. On the basis of widely documented research, it appears that this alienation and feeling that "no one cares" arise from lack of positive connections with the community (Education Commission of the States [ECS], 1999).

Much has been written about the internal and external risk factors that enable violent behavior: access to weapons, violent movies and videos, school instability, psychopathology, victimization, and upheaval in homes and neighborhoods. Today, the emphasis is shifting away from individual pathology and remediation to an emphasis on resilience and prevention. A public health approach to youth violence (US Department of Health and Human Services, 2001) asks the questions: What factors protect students from risk? What can schools and communities do to nurture youth and prevent violent behavior?

Several school, community, family, peer, and personal developmental assets are receiving attention as possible protective factors in reducing the risk of violent behavior (School Mental Health Project, 1999):

- clarity of norms and rules about behavior;
- linkages to community;
- commitment and attachment to school;
- positive academic performance;
- social and emotional competence;

- bonding to family; and
- attachment to prosocial others.

Positive educational experiences promote coping skills and help students understand how they can recover from stressful environments. School psychologists and counselors can assist in creating a culture of caring in which students experience the needed structure and emotional support to overcome risk factors. Service learning helps students' develop protective social, emotional, and academic assets to counteract violence. A collateral benefit may be that rather than viewing students as "problems," the community may instead come to view students as resources to help solve problems of violence and its consequences (Benard, 1990).

Service learning can be an effective means of meeting the goals of No Child Left Behind (NCLB) and the Title IV program to promote safe schools that support academic achievement and encourage drug-free and nonviolent lifestyles (RMC Research Corporation, n.d.). The "Safe and Drug-Free Schools and Communities Act" supports service learning by providing funds for schools to implement drug and violence prevention activities that may include community service and service-learning projects and by allowing funds to be used for service-learning projects that are designed to rebuild safe and healthy neighborhoods and increase students' sense of individual responsibility. Through service learning, students become part of the safe schools solution (Hill, 1996).

Service-learning projects do not necessarily have to deal with violence-related issues to have a violence prevention effect. However, connections between community service-learning projects can be made to various social studies curricula that address challenging problems such as societal violence. Students should be encouraged to reflect upon the needs of victims of violence and to plan strategies to assist victims in rebuilding their personal resiliency. Victimization is among the risk factors impeding healthy development (National Center for Victims of Crime, 2005). Hess (1997) recommended that service learning, as part of a comprehensive school-based violence prevention program, focuses on reducing known risk factors for violence by enhancing known protective factors. An essential ingredient in any service-learning projects dealing with violence prevention is the firm expectation of respectful interpersonal interactions and nonviolent behavior.

The experience of Putnam Vocational Technical High School showed how service learning can impact students and facilitate the development of a positive school climate (Gonzalez, Wagner, & Brunton, 1993). At Putnam, the faculty, community members, parents, and students effected a dramatic transformation in moving a violence-riddled school toward becoming a high-performing school in just five years. Students used their technical and academic skills in a variety of service projects to make improvements in the school and in the community at large. Pre- and post-service-learning data are striking (ECS, 1999): Discipline referrals and dropout rates decreased while grade point averages and plans for postsecondary increased.

Youth courts are an innovative service-learning alternative to traditional juvenile courts to address the needs of at-risk populations (Pearson, 2006; Pearson & Jurich, 2005). Sometimes referred to as teen courts or peer juries, youth courts are a restorative justice program that helps offenders rebuild relationships with their community (National Youth Court Center, 2005). Youth courts handle cases involving violent behavior, such as assault, disorderly conduct, and interfering with the peace at school. There is judicial oversight to this process. Youth volunteers are trained to serve as attorneys to try youth offenders in front of a jury of their peers and in some cases, a teenage judge. These court proceedings capitalize on peer pressure to encourage the offender to reform. Community service is the most frequent sentencing option employed in 99% of the cases.

Youth courts embrace service learning to teach young people about the law and their civic responsibilities. Service on youth courts easily connects with academic learning objectives in civics or social studies and also provides an opportunity for career exploration for both the youth court volunteers and the offenders sentenced to community service. Students increase their understanding of the law, the reason for the law, and the consequences of breaking the law.

Youth courts are a promising prevention strategy. According to the Urban Institute's Evaluation of Teen Courts Project, which was based on four teen court programs studied in four different states (Alaska, Maryland, Arizona, and Missouri), the six-month recidivism figures among the programs ranged from 6% to 9% (National Youth Court Center, 2005).

Stopping Youth Violence through Service Learning produced by Youth Service America is a compendium of service-learning project ideas that address the issue of school violence (see http://www.ysa.org/nysd/pdf_file/violence_module.pdf). The document provides links to information on various aspects of youth violence and related resources, such as bullying, gangs, guns, youth courts and juvenile justice, conflict resolution, and violence prevention.

The problem of violence in schools and communities is complex. Service learning is certainly not a cure-all for the multitude of issues raised by violence. However, the personal, social, career, and academic benefits of service learning in promoting positive youth development recommend its use as a component of violence prevention programs.

Crisis Intervention

In recent years, our global community has suffered the effects of terrorism and several major natural disasters. The magnitude of these disasters impelled many people to contribute in some way to relief efforts. For many people, these contributions were an important coping mechanism. Certainly, children and adolescents were affected by what they saw happening in this country and around the world. However, there were fewer outlets for youth to have a legitimate role in the healing process. The prevailing view is that children are the helpless victims of a crisis rather than resources to help with recovery efforts when disasters occur. Service learning can make crisis intervention a *teachable* moment (Gross & Kielsmeier, 2006) that goes beyond charity to empower students in making a difference in their local, national, and global communities.

The website for Institute for Global Education and Service-Learning (www.igesl.org) contains information about service-learning programs to involve youth in crisis intervention. *Learning Through Service—Strengthening the Homeland* is a service-learning program designed to increase awareness of the need for emergency preparedness and disaster education supported by student activities in their schools, homes, and communities. *Youth Organized for Disaster Action* (Y.O.D.A.) is another service-learning program that helps students to prepare their families, schools, and communities for unexpected emergencies and disasters. Students met various curriculum goals while they:

- prepared and distributed emergency kits in their community,
- assessed the security and safety needs of the community,
- created emergency plans for their homes and schools,
- researched the effect of disasters on communities,
- learned first aid,
- taught others how to prepare for and respond to emergencies,
- wrote stories to help younger children understand what to do in an emergency,
- developed guidelines for ensuring the safety of pets during emergencies,
- produced public service announcements about disaster preparedness,
- organized health and safety fairs, and
- helped victims of local disasters.

Planning crisis intervention and management programs are also opportunities for multicultural education. Because service learning connects to communities, diversity issues at the global as well as at the local levels can be addressed. Students learn how the customs, rituals, and social relationships of various cultural groups are important considerations to enable the community to cope with a crisis. One component of a service-learning crisis intervention project could involve students identifying the specific culture-related needs of the community during times of crisis, such as access to interpreters, religious figures, and healers (Athey & Moody-Williams, 2003).

Crises within schools have unique features because of a school's organizational structure and sense of community. A crisis at school can undermine the stability of the entire system. Crises that specifically affect the school community include suicide, death, and medical emergencies as well as incidents of violence. Through service-learning projects, students of all ages can be enlisted to assist with crisis prevention, management, and recovery efforts. For example, students can be taught how to offer support to their peers during a crisis. Service can help children and adolescents learn to put their own problems in perspective and to think beyond themselves to help others in a time of need. School psychologists and counselors should be involved in crisis intervention/management (Allen et al., 2002; Heath & Sheen, 2005; Poland, Pitcher, & Lazarus, 2002) and engage students as participants on those teams.

References

Allen, M., Burt, K., Bryan, E., Carter, D., Orsi, R., & Dukan, L. (2002). School counselors' preparation for and participation in crisis intervention. *Professional School Counseling, 6,* 96–102.

Athey, J., & Moody-Williams, J. (2003). *Developing cultural competence in disaster mental health programs: Guiding principles and recommendations.* Washington, DC: US Department of Health and Human Services. Retrieved April 17, 2006, from http://media.shs.net/ken/pdf/SMA03-3828/CulturalCompetence_FINALwithcovers.pdf.

Benard, B. (1990). *Youth Service: From youth as problems to youth as resources.* Portland, OR: Northwest Regional Educational Laboratory.

Education Commission of the States [ECS] (1999, December). *Service-learning: An educational strategy for preventing school violence.* Denver, CO: Author.

Gonzalez, J., Wagner, F.W., & Brunton, D. (1993). Community service-learning at Putnam High School. *Equity & Excellence in Education, 26*(2), 27–29.

Gross, T., & Kielsmeier, J.C. (2006). Resources for recovery: Young people, service, learning, and disasters. *Growing to greatness: The state of service-learning project.* St. Paul, MN: National Youth Leadership Council.

Heath, M.A., & Sheen, D. (2005). *School-based crisis intervention: Preparing all personnel to assist.* New York: Guilford.

Hess, D. (1997). Violence prevention and service-learning. *Social Education, 61,* 279–281.

Hill, M.S. (1996, April). Making students part of the safe schools solution. *NASSP Bulletin,* 80(579), 24–30.

Horatio Alger Association. (2005). *The state of our nation's youth.* Alexandria, VA: Author. Retrieved April 5, 2006, from http://www.horatioalger.com/pdfs/state05.pdf.

National Center for Victims of Crime. (2005). *Reaching and serving teen victims: A practical handbook.* Washington, DC: Author.

National Youth Court Center. (2005). *Facts and stats.* Retrieved April 11, 2006, from http://www.youthcourt.net.

Pearson, S. (2006). Youth courts: An alternative to traditional juvenile courts. In *Growing to greatness: The state of service-learning project* (pp. 46–52). St. Paul, MN: National Youth Leadership Council.

Pearson, S., & Jurich, S. (2005). *Youth court: A community solution for embracing at-risk youth—A national update.* Washington, DC: American Youth Policy Forum. Retrieved April 11, 2006, from http://www.youthcourt.net/Publications/Alpha.htm.

Poland, S., Pitcher, G., & Lazarus, P.M. (2002). Best practices in crisis prevention and management. In A. Thomas & J. Grimes (Eds.), *Best practices in school psychology—IV* (pp. 1057–1079). Bethesda, MD: National Association of School Psychologists.

RMC Research Corporation. (n.d.). *Service-learning & No Child Left Behind Act of 2001: Title IV, safe and drug-free schools and communities.* Retrieved April 6, 2006, from http://www.rmcdenver.com/Title%20IV%20Final%20proof.pdf.

School Mental Health Project. (Summer, 1999). Youth suicide/depression/violence. *Addressing Barriers to Learning, 4*(1). Retrieved April 6, 2006, from http://smhp.psych.ucla.edu/news.htm.

US Department of Health and Human Services. (2001). *Youth violence: A report of the Surgeon General.* Washington, DC: Author. Retrieved April 6, 2006, from http://www.mentalhealth.samhsa.gov/youthviolence/surgeongeneral/SG_Site.

US Department of Health and Human Services. (2003). *Child Health USA.* Washington, DC: Author. Retrieved April 5, 2006, from http://www.mchb.hrsa.gov/chusa03/pages/status_adolescents.htm.

Section III
Service-Learning Blueprints to Build Developmental Assets

This section provides a pre-K-12 service-learning curriculum and describes how school-based mental health professionals can adopt and adapt such a program in their own work. Exemplars, or "blueprints," of service-learning activities within general education classrooms at the preschool, elementary, middle, and high school levels are presented. In each case, there are explanations of how the service activity can be modified to meet the needs of students with disabilities. The components of service learning can be conceptualized as building blocks to foster developmental assets:

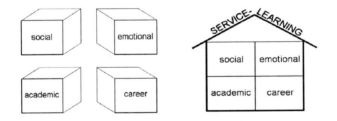

Here is an example: Middle school students collect paper to be recycled from each classroom in their school. The students could weigh how much paper is collected each week. They might determine what percentage came from each classroom and graph the results, to connect the service to the math curriculum standards. They might write letters to local officials asking them to expand the school recycling program. This type of advocacy is compatible with the state standards for English language arts. They might study the history of recycling and learn that it dates back to ancient Rome, linking the service to the social studies' curriculum standards. They might explore careers associated with recycling. Students would work collaboratively, negotiating interpersonal issues

109

and planning how to accomplish their goals. Throughout the project, students reflect on their service experiences and broader issues, such as the need for recycling to preserve natural resources. It is easy to imagine myriad connections that can be made between a service activity and social, emotional, career, and academic curriculum standards. Thus, service learning enables students to see the relationships among disciplines, to experience interpersonal growth through collaboration, and to recognize the link between learning in school and living in the real world.

An important point to keep in mind is that service learning is not just community service. Raising money to benefit hurricane Katrina victims is community service, but it is not service learning because the fund-raising has no connection to the curriculum. For this community service to become service learning, students might analyze the data concerning funding sources, to connect to the math standards. They might write an advocacy piece for the local newspaper to generate interest in giving, to connect to the English language arts standards. They might study hurricanes and their effect on the land and people, to connect to the science and technology standards. They could examine the politics of relief efforts, to connect to the social studies curriculum. Students could hone career and employability skills such as fund-raising, promotion, marketing, organizing, and problem solving, as well as gain exposure to the field of meteorology or the complexities of governmental bureaucracies in emergency planning. They could reflect upon the power of giving and the responsibility of each person to the good of all. These are some of the many ways for community service to become service learning.

Service can take place within the school or in the community outside. The previous examples describe in-school projects; however, there are numerous ways of performing service in the outside community. For example, students studying the water cycle in science class could take a field trip to collect water samples from a local source, test the water for pollutants, analyze the results, and present their findings to the local water board.

Curriculum Scope and Sequence

Service learning offers the kind of educational opportunities that can produce well-rounded graduates who are both educated and caring. It would be ideal to foster these experiences from the very first days of school and carry them through to the day of high school graduation. Many people associate "service" with students of high school age. Certainly, older students have a greater range of service project options, owing to their greater maturity, wider set of capabilities, less need for supervision, and the ability to transport themselves to service sites independently. However, a commitment to serving others and the development of values begins much earlier in life, and these ideals continue to be challenged or reinforced through adulthood. Research suggests that taking a developmental perspective in regard to service-learning programs is optimal, because young children who volunteer are more likely to continue to do so when they become teenagers, and teens who serve are more likely to carry on the habit as adults. A pre-K-12 service-learning program offers ongoing opportunities for children to serve and to embrace a lifelong ethic of service to others (Search Institute, 2000).

A service-learning curriculum can be developed to address the learning needs and requirements of preschoolers to high school seniors. In this way, service becomes an integral part of the school experience and part of students' personal lives. A cohesive pre-K-12 curriculum affords the school district an opportunity to integrate its service-learning program so that one level informs the next. Each year of the service-learning program can build on the information and skills acquired in the earlier years. Therefore, it is useful to have a theme in a district-wide service-learning program. This section presents a plan that can cover an entire pre-K-12 system, using the environment as a sample unifying theme and service to provide an authentic learning context. However, it is suggested that you start small—at the grassroots level—one student, one group, or one classroom at a time. The district-wide example is meant to show "the big picture," that is, how a pre-K-12 service-learning program might ultimately be realized.

Aligning with the Academic Mission

Sometimes mental health professionals within schools can feel isolated from the academic mission of the school. There are times when it seems as though counseling or special education is regarded as an add-on, while the spotlight is placed on regular education teachers and what goes on in general education classrooms. Perhaps this is because psychological and counseling services are not always integrated with the school's primary academic mission. Often, school psychologists and counselors work outside the classroom, in offices, as if social and emotional learning could be segmented from other kinds of learning and only take place in a counselor's office. Moreover, school psychologists and counselors are key players in developing academic interventions but do not always play a role in their implementation, particularly in general education classrooms.

Yet *No Child Left Behind* makes it very clear that closing the achievement gap must be the top priority of *all* school personnel. In the light of current school reform, everyone working in a school must share accountability for the academic achievement of students. School improvement plans focus on moving academic performance data in a positive direction. It is critical for *all* school personnel to work toward positively impacting student achievement (Dahir & Stone, 2003). To meet this challenge, things need to be done differently. Like all changes, service learning requires moving out of a comfort zone to pursue goals for students in a different way. The payoff will come in eliminating the achievement gap, positioning school psychology and counseling as central to the academic mission of the school, and increasing job satisfaction. So, how does this work?

Because service learning can be used by the entire student body, it gives a context for working together with general education classroom teachers on a number of levels—as a consultant helping a teacher plan a service-learning curriculum, as a co-teacher in a service-learning class, or as a specialist working with a small group of students within the service-learning class. Service learning also can be conducted by school psychologists or counselors outside of class, working with a student or a group of students on a service project that is tied to specific social, emotional, career, or academic curriculum goals. Because school-based mental health professionals know the positive developmental outcomes of service learning, they can work on a larger scale as catalysts for a district to adopt a system-wide service-learning program. Some districts have created the position of Service-Learning Coordinator to develop and manage system-wide programs. Indeed, school psychologists and counselors are uniquely positioned to infuse a service-learning program with social/emotional learning, career exploration, and academic goal interventions, making them a natural choice to fulfill such a coordinator role.

Administrators also need to know that service learning is a recommended strategy to address the mandates of the federal *No Child Left Behind Act*. As such, it is not an "add-on" but directly addresses the mission of the school. Service learning engages students in learning, offers an integrating context for all subject matter, provides opportunities for social, emotional, and career education, and supports the goal of optimal academic achievement for all. Moreover, service learning also supports the professional guidelines for best practice set forth by the National Association of School Psychologists (NASP) and the American School Counselor Association (ASCA), which call for scientifically-based and ethically sound practice.

The sample curriculum included in this section illustrates the comprehensive ability of service learning to support social, emotional, career, and academic goals, as well as to accommodate students with special needs. First, a service-learning program for students in general education settings will be described. Modifications to the general education service-learning program will then be discussed to show how to meet the needs of students with disabilities who are working with school psychologists and counselors. Finally, a model of teamwork will be proposed to facilitate collaboration with special education teachers, speech/language pathologists, occupational therapists, and other specialists to integrate and achieve multiple goals through one program. Thus, service learning offers a new approach to collaboration through authentic learning contexts for students and educators alike.

Environment as a Theme

The environment is one example of an area that lends itself to service learning. There are countless other possible themes, such as nutrition, health, social justice issues of hunger and homelessness, poverty, immigration, literacy, or improving community safety. A theme is useful because it offers a way to integrate projects and curriculum within a school and within a district. Using an environmental theme of recycling, for example, preschoolers can sort recyclable materials and later, in third grade, they can find uses for recyclables. When the children reach middle school, they can develop a recycling program for their cafeteria. In high school, students can advocate for a community-wide recycling program.

This sample curriculum focuses on the environment because environmental problems can be found everywhere; indeed, solving environmental problems is imperative as evidence continues to build that human-induced global warming seriously threatens our world (Hansen, 2004; Mitchell, Loew, Wood & Vellinga, 2006; Oppenheimer, 1998). Projects involving the environment also give children and adolescents an opportunity to see firsthand the effect each person has on the immediate community and the world as a whole. They can recognize that each person and each home plays a significant role in contributing to the release of carbon dioxide into the atmosphere through the use of appliances, electronics, and automobiles. Personal choices end up affecting the entire planet. Global warming may be the critical issue of our time. Can schools afford *not* to focus on environmental issues?

A study of 40 schools using the environment as a unifying theme in education indicated that it was an effective vehicle for delivering higher academic achievement, decreasing discipline problems, improving attendance, and gener-ating greater enthusiasm toward school (Lieberman & Hoody, 1998). Research from a study funded by the Corporation for National Service (Madigan, 2000) to explore environmental service learning in over 100 school programs found a number of benefits, including the engagement of students who had not typically flourished in the classroom, the potential to draw parental interest and partic-ipation, increased self-esteem and the development of positive self-concept in students, an integrated context for learning, multiple opportunities for long-term partnerships with the community, the establishment of positive adult–youth experiences that may be otherwise missing from students' lives, and projects with visible, tangible results. In addition, teachers interviewed for the study often cited the benefits of the many hands-on activities for youth at risk for school failure through what one described as our "most accessible" resource, the environment (Madigan, 2000).

It is not surprising that the environment is cited as an area with the potential to engage student, faculty, parent, and community interest. After all, the environment is everyone's home. Because we all have a stake in its future, there is an emotional component shared throughout communities that generates interest in activities that address an authentic need to protect or improve the environment. This is an important point to keep in mind as you consider a theme for your service-learning projects. Community support may translate to financial support of schools during times of budget crises. Environmental service projects very often yield tangible results that entire communities can see and from which all can benefit.

There is little question that environmental projects have many "academic" components. Hands-on, concrete experiments generate data for mathematical and scientific study. Environmental issues can be the focus of language arts classes, with a wealth of opportunities for reading, written expression, and discussion. Environmental concerns are intertwined with historical and sociological issues of industry, agriculture, use of the land, and so on. Ecological issues are immersed in political, legal, and ethical debate—including animal rights, placement of landfills, exploitation of natural resources, and disposal of toxic waste. Because the topic of the environment can be appreciated on both concrete and abstract levels, it can be incorporated into preschool through high school curricula. The diversity of environmental issues supports multiple learning situations and multiple learning styles.

Positive Personal Development

But what about social and emotional learning? How do service-learning projects relating to environmental concerns nurture positive personal and interpersonal development? Guidelines for effective social and emotional education suggest that programs target four domains. First, students need to build life skills and social competencies as well as understand what promotes their health and prevents problems. Next, the transitions and crises young people may face in life require coping skills and a system of social support. Finally, positive contributory service is cited as integral to helping students become knowledgeable, responsible, and caring (Elias et al., 1997).

Service learning reinforces skills in each domain of social and emotional learning. The service-learning curriculum proposed here inherently supports the development of life skills and social competencies by bringing people together in natural contexts. It requires that people work together to solve a problem. Interpersonal interaction is a necessity, as is group decision-making and sharing of skills and information. Moreover, the service-learning activities enhance time management capabilities, organizational know-how, and encourage students to take responsibility for their actions. Students of this environmentally-based service-learning curricula learn the effect each of us has on the earth as a whole. The environmental aspect underscores the need to be caretakers of the planet, to be cognizant of health issues and take action to reduce the effects of pollution and to prevent further damage by addressing conditions such as global warming. Because the service-learning program is one in which students work together, a feeling of teamwork and camaraderie is supported, offering social support in times when things go wrong or when difficulties are encountered. Also, school psychologists and counselors working with students in a service-learning project, as opposed to within traditional counseling situations, are able to teach and reinforce coping skills as the students grapple with the frustrations inherent in problem-solving or in dealing with troubling interpersonal interactions, all within an *authentic* context. Finally, the service component of service learning guarantees that students experience the gratification that comes with making a meaningful contribution to their community. Moreover, the ethical dilemmas associated with environmental issues provide a rich context for students and teachers to explore moral questions and nurture higher order thinking skills.

Within the word "environment" is the Latin word "viron" meaning circle. Through reflections, students learn to appreciate the circularity, or interconnectedness, of the ecosystems of earth and themselves. As environmentalist John Muir wrote, "When we try to pick anything out by itself, we find it hitched to everything else in the Universe" (Muir, 1988, p. 110). The circular nature of things will be reflected in the curriculum, where real-life connections are made between what students learn and the world they inhabit. Students can carry on this appreciation as they become adult members of society, and develop an identity grounded in mutual responsibility (Saltmarsh, 1997).

A useful source for service-learning projects with an environmental theme is Project WILD. Project WILD is the result of a partnership between state fish and wildlife agencies and natural resource professionals. This organization offers a complete K-12 curriculum focusing on wildlife and their habitats and another complete K-12 curriculum that centers on aquatic wildlife and aquatic ecosystems, as well as a variety of training workshops for both curricula. The objective of Project WILD is to engage students in meaningful and purposeful service to their school and community. For more information, go to www.projectwild.org.

There are a number of other sources of project curricula relating to the environment. Explore the following websites for additional curriculum ideas: The Environmental Literacy Council (for the topic of air quality): http://www.enviroliteracy.org/subcategory.php/178.html; Center for Global Environmental Education—Watershed Action: http://www.cgee.hamline.edu/watershed/action/projects/index.htm; Audubon Society: Education: http://www.audubon.org/educate/index.html; Natural Resources Defense Council (for renewable/alternative sources of energy/sustainable development): http://www.nrdc.org/greengate/ guides/driving.asp.

Blueprints

This section contains several "blueprints" relating to various service activities. Separate blueprints for preschool, elementary, middle, and high school students describe a service-learning experience for students at those grade levels who are learning in general education classrooms. In each case, the blueprint provides a description of the service activity, samples of state curriculum standards supported by the activity, the service provided, activities for reflection, the service learning that is taking place, and a list of developmental assets supported by the experience. The blueprints reflect curriculum standards set forth by the Massachusetts Department of Education (1999, 2000, 2001ab, 2003, 2004, 2005ab, 2006) and are intended to serve as a representation of how state standards relate to the service activity. The blueprints are not meant to be exhaustive in detail, but rather offer a framework of how service activities relate to the academic curriculum, an outline of the social/emotional learning benefits for students, and a consideration of the community benefit, whether it be internal to the school or involving outside recipients.

For Students with Disabilities

Each blueprint describing a service-learning activity for a given grade level is followed by a chart showing how that activity could be modified to be used with students who have disabilities. These charts list disability categories, describe how the service is modified for each, provide tips on working with students in each disability area, and suggest ways to collaborate with other educators or specialists.

For Gifted Students

Academically gifted students often have time on their hands in a classroom, owing to their ability to finish class work quickly and competently. These students can use this extra time to explore areas within the service-learning project that are of particular interest to them. There are a number of options for the classroom teacher to keep these students motivated by offering "vertical" enrichment activities that challenge them, rather than simply giving them "more of the same." These activities may include such things as asking them to invent a new type of composting bin or to plan a new system of recycling. The students could be assigned to work with a community mentor in a field related to the environment in their area of interest. Students with other talents might use their special abilities to support the environmental project in some other way, for example to create artwork or music about the environment.

Youth Voice and Project Ownership

In each case, it is preferable that the students have a voice in selecting the service activity. Student ownership increases the sense of meaningfulness and personal investment in the project. If it is not feasible to have students select the service project, they should be given substantial roles in the planning, implementation, and evaluation of the project. Students need to be instructed prior to the start of the project as to what constitutes appropriate behavior during the activity and to understand what is expected of them.

The Big Picture: Blueprints and Modifications for Pre-K-12 Service Learning

At the conclusion of this section, you will find a set of blueprints for an environmentally-based service-learning program for preschool, elementary, middle, and high school students learning in general education classrooms, as well as charts showing how to modify the activity for students with disabilities.

The following is an illustration of a middle school service-learning activity. The ideas presented for middle school students can easily be extrapolated up or down for students at other grade levels.

Taking a Closer Look: Service Learning at the Middle School Level

What makes service learning appropriate at the middle school level? Middle school youth are experiencing dramatic emotional and physical changes. Cognitive development at this age can include the beginning of inferential and abstract thinking. Cognizant of the physical and developmental changes of early adolescence, the National Commission on Resources for Youth (Schine, Shoup, & Harrington, 1981) recommended that schools develop programs that enable middle school students to test and discover new skills; to develop a sense of competence that can serve as an antidote to the self-doubt that can characterize this period; to take on different roles; to be exposed to a variety of adult role models, representing different backgrounds and occupations; to speak and have their ideas heard; to examine their values in authentic contexts; to participate in activities that have tangible outcomes; and to take part in decision making.

There is a close connection between educational philosophy and practice at the middle school level and the goals of service learning (Schukar, 1997). One of the principal objectives of the middle school educational experience is to provide student-centered learning opportunities that encourage student responsibility for learning. The following blueprint covers a service-learning activity intended for grade six students learning in a general education classroom:

Blueprint

Middle School Grade Six General Education Classroom Activity: "Tracking the Trash"

Tasks

Students will learn how much food is thrown away at their school each day and use the information to educate other students and inform a cafeteria recycling program by:

- recording the number of students at their lunch table, the number of foil, paper, cans, bottles, juice boxes, milk cartons, and plastic utensils per student each day for one month,
- asking students to pour any leftover milk into empty gallon containers and record daily amounts,
- totaling each category, as well as determining a ratio of trash items to student on a monthly basis,

- illustrating data on bar graphs and pie charts, and determining mean, mode, median, maximum and minimum, and range for each trash category,
- interviewing the cafeteria manager to learn what foods are thrown away, what happens to leftovers, and what governmental guidelines must be followed in planning and packaging meals, and
- presenting findings and making recommendations in a school-wide assembly to fellow students, faculty, and parents.

Reflection activities will require students to understand the elements of a system, to explore the theme of perspective, and to analyze information and use evidence in making an argument.

Essential Questions Posed for Social/Emotional Growth

- What is the responsibility of a person to the environment?
- What are the ethics of environmental protection?
- Does a person have a moral responsibility to engage others in protecting the environment?
- What is the attitude of other students in the school about recycling in the cafeteria?
- How can a more environmentally responsible climate be encouraged at the school?
- How did the group cooperate to solve problems?
- What was fun about the project? What was frustrating?

Links to the Curriculum Standards

In this example, the environmental service-learning activity is designed to provide an authentic context to help students achieve social, emotional, career, and academic curriculum standards as set forth by the Massachusetts Department of Education. The Massachusetts Department of Education curriculum frameworks also intend that civility and character education be integrated with the academic curriculum. School psychologists and school counselors are the key personnel in promoting standards concerning mental health, interpersonal relationships, civility, and character education. The following list is not exhaustive but representative of the various relevant curriculum standards.

DOE Curriculum Standard	Description
Math Standard 6 for Data Analysis, Statistics, and Probability	describe and compare data sets using median, mean, mode, maximum, minimum, and range; construct line plots and circle graphs

English Language Arts Standard 2 for Questioning, Listening, and Contributing	gather information through interviews
English Language Arts Standard 3 for Oral Presentations	showing appropriate changes in delivery (gestures, vocabulary, pace, visuals) and using language for dramatic effect
English Language Arts Standard 23 for Organizing Ideas in Writing	placement of details, logical order, organizing information
Health Standard 13 for Ecological Health	describe how business and individuals can work together to solve ecological health problems, such as conserving natural resources and decreasing pollution
Science and Technology Standard 5	explain the elements of a system: goals, inputs, processes, outputs, and feedback
English Language Arts Standard 11 for Themes in Reading and Literature	analyze and evaluate themes; distinguish theme from topic
English Language Arts Standard 13	analyze and use evidence in making an argument
Mental Health Standard 5 for Decision-Making	**explain and practice a model for decision-making that includes gathering information, predicting outcomes, identifying moral implications, and evaluating outcomes**
Mental Health Standard 5 for Coping Skills	**explain how skills such as perceiving situations as opportunities, taking action, and exerting control positively influence self-concept**
Mental Health Standard 5 for Identity Development	**describe the effects of leadership skills on the promotion of teamwork**
Mental Health Standard 5 for Emotional Growth	**apply methods to accommodate a variety of feelings in a constructive way**
Interpersonal Relationships Standard 7 for Communication	**apply both verbal and non-verbal communication skills to develop positive relationships and improve the social environment of the school**

Reflection Activities:

- Preservice reflection through discussion: what do students predict as an outcome? Do they think this activity will change their own beliefs and habits? Why or why not?
- Daily journal entries on use of disposable versus reusable containers and recording of changes in thought and habits.
- Daily group discussion of teamwork and interpersonal problems encountered.
- Explore ethical dilemmas.

- Group discussion following final presentation of results (processing and conclusions); ideas for future projects.

Services Provided:

- Education of students on the subject of environmentally responsible behavior.
- Production of data to inform a school cafeteria recycling program.
- Reduction of trash sent to landfill.

Service Learning:

- Increasing awareness of personal habits in regard to generation of waste.
- Learning personal responsibility for the environment.
- Understanding the effect each person has on the environment.
- Seeing the relationship of personal choices to group outcomes.
- Participating in collaborative problem solving and teamwork.
- Appreciating community.
- Applying academic skills in an authentic context.

Career Connections:

- Reporter
- Researcher
- Mathematician
- Writer
- Politician
- Marketing/public relations representative
- Financial analyst
- Coach
- Educator

Developmental Assets Supported:

- External: Caring school climate; youth as resources; service to others; high expectations
- Internal: Achievement motivation; school engagement; bonding to school; caring; responsibility; planning and decision making; personal power; self-esteem; sense of purpose

Meeting Curriculum Standards

In this case, the students have chosen an activity called "Tracking the Trash." Through this activity, students will learn how much food is thrown away at their school each day. They will use the information generated by their study to educate other students regarding recycling and implement a cafeteria recycling program.

Specifically, students will work together to record the number of students at their lunch table, the number of foil, paper, cans, bottles, juice boxes, milk cartons, and plastic utensils per student per day for one month. Students involved in the recycling project will ask other students to pour any leftover milk into empty gallon containers and record daily amounts. At the end of the month, students will total each category, and determine a ratio of trash items to student. They will illustrate the data on bar and line graphs, as well as pie charts, and will determine mean, mode, median, maximum and minimum ranges for each trash category. Students will interview the cafeteria manager to learn what foods are thrown away, what happens to leftovers, and what governmental guidelines must be followed in planning and packaging meals. The students will compile their findings in individual written reports; the class will decide on recommendations to the school and a committee of students will be chosen to present results at a school-wide assembly to fellow students, faculty, and parents.

This activity is particularly salient to the social, emotional, career, and academic learning needs of sixth-grade students. In math, the state curriculum frameworks indicate that sixth grade students are required to learn how to analyze data. They must be able to describe and compare data sets using median, mode, maximum, minimum, and the range. In addition, they are required to know how to construct line plots and pie charts. In English language arts, they are asked to be able to gather information by interviewing people; they must be able to deliver oral presentations, showing appropriate changes in delivery, using gestures, vocabulary, pace, and visuals; they are required to organize their ideas in writing by placing details correctly and putting information in a logical order. The state curriculum standards for health and career call for sixth graders to be able to understand how business and individuals can work together to solve ecological problems, such as conserving natural resources and decreasing pollution. The standards for mental health focus on identity issues, responsible decision-making, communication, emotional regulation, and interpersonal skills that are all required in carrying out the service-learning project.

Note that these are just a few of the social, emotional, career, and academic standards that can be applied to this activity. They are provided here as examples of the many possible learning tie-ins to the service activity. It is easy to see how this service activity, by addressing a genuine need, makes the curriculum come alive. Students can readily understand why it is important to know how to collect and analyze data. They can experience the empowerment that comes when they are given a forum where their ideas can be heard. They acquire the skills needed for collaboration and teamwork. They learn how to manage conflict. They discover the value of being able to communicate clearly and logically, and the value of their work to the community. Thus, the integrated nature of service with the curriculum reflects the essence of the middle school philosophy that the organization of the curriculum should encompass all subject areas.

Fundamental to the philosophy of middle school education, but frequently missing from traditional middle school science programs, is the notion that scientific concepts be understood in relation to relevant social issues, as well as to personal decision-making goals and career awareness (Bybee et al., 1990). In our sample environmentally-based preK-12 service-learning program, preschool students learn about landfills. In grade three, they come to understand the difference between a landfill and composting as a method to dispose of food wastes, and they create a compost pile. Now in middle school, they explore the recycling of food containers and related cafeteria trash. They are able to connect their individual actions with community outcomes, and understand the contribution that scientific knowledge makes to the resolution of social problems. They are able to recognize the relationship of personal decisions to the unnecessary contribution of recyclables to the landfill, and of the ensuing impact on the land. They can draw conclusions about the responsibilities of everyone, including the cafeteria manager as well as school staff and students, in environmental stewardship. They learn to negotiate and resolve conflicts as they collaborate on the project.

Civic Awareness

The recycling service-learning activity promotes student civic awareness and engagement. It begins with a democratic process of service activity selection. The service is a classroom community decision. The outcome of the activity supports student understanding of the idea of working toward a common good through active participation in the community. Students design a school recycling program. They participate in the process of looking at community problems and developing solutions and plans of action. The process of creating a plan for recycling in the school fosters an understanding of the decision-making process inherent in the democratic system. It prepares students to become active in the community by reinforcing skills such as fact finding, negotiation, problem-solving, and coming to consensus, all within an ethic of service.

Career Development

As students take on various roles in this service-learning activity, such as group leader, spokesperson for the class, interviewer/reporter, writer, scientist, mathematician, researcher, politician, they are able to get a taste of various careers. There are many "hats" a student can wear through this one service-learning activity and many ways to reinforce different skills through different job assignments. They also have an opportunity to closely observe and, in some cases, actually perform adult occupations. A student might learn that he or she is quite comfortable talking in front of a group and may be empowered to consider a career within the law, education, politics, or business. Another student may dislike public speaking but may really enjoy interviewing people. Perhaps a career in journalism or writing would appeal. Still another may find it is fun to collect and analyze data, bringing to mind jobs in computer science, the natural sciences, or the financial services industry. There are virtually endless connections students can make between service experiences and career paths.

Moreover, this service-learning activity supports workplace competencies recognized by the state of Massachusetts Department of Education. For example, it supports literacy and communication skills through the interviewing task, generating a written report, and an oral presentation. Students sharpen their ability to organize and analyze data by collecting and sorting their findings on cafeteria refuse, obtaining information from the cafeteria manager, and using their knowledge to offer real solutions. The experience fosters the ability to initiate and complete projects, as this is a start-to-finish project that also addresses time management skills because students must collect the trash and record the trash data within the confines of the lunch period. It supports the ability to accept direction and criticism, a component close to the school and workplace experience, and encourages the ability to interact positively with others because it requires cooperative group work with peers, as well as prosocial interaction with adults. Finally, the project instills a sense of taking responsibility for life choices because it gives students an opportunity to take on different roles that can help them make more informed career decisions.

Social and Emotional Learning

At 11 or 12 years of age, students' social and emotional concerns include the development of self-esteem, social competence, leadership skills, and self-efficacy. As they contribute through service to the good of the school and of the community beyond, significant social and emotional learning takes place. The community comes to regard the students as a valuable resource in themselves, bolstering self-esteem. The students develop a sense of competence by using their math skills to determine the status of trash and food disposal in the school and inform a recycling program. Their self-confidence grows as they realize that they can make a difference in the world. The students must work together on the project to achieve mutual goals, fostering leadership and team building capabilities. The project also supports moral development and a value structure as students grapple with questions such as "What is the responsibility of a person to the environment?" "Does a person have a moral responsibility to engage others in protecting the environment?" "What are the ethics of environmental protection?" "How do politics impact environmental concerns?" They begin to see the complexities inherent to social issues and social reform.

Reflection as a Learning Tool

Reflection is imperative in service learning because it is the phase in which the actual learning takes place. Although the old maxim "Experience is the best teacher" suggests that merely doing something is enough to learn from it, research and personal observation indicates that this is not true. Reflection involves making observations, asking questions, pondering experiences in a way that enables a person to come to new understandings and ways of thinking. In this way, reflection provides feedback to correct previous errors, feeding a continuous cycle of learning. There are many theories concerning the stages involved in learning (Dewey, 1938; Kolb 1984; Schon, 1983) but common among many is the necessity of a cycle. Such "experiential learning cycle" theories vary in the number of stages cited, but center around the basic tenet that learning is the result of experience, reflection, concluding, and planning. Thus, reflection is an essential component of learning.

Reflection is not a new concept to school psychologists and counselors. When students are referred for discipline problems, they are often encouraged to think about their actions and reflect on what they might have done differently in a given situation. Reflection is also an important skill for students experiencing academic problems, who often do not analyze their work or habits to learn about themselves as students. They often cannot say what is going wrong for them in the classroom.

Reflection is considered "the learning in service-learning" (Eyler & Giles, 1999). Reflection enables students to become aware of changes in themselves and it gives them a sense of empowerment by showing them the ability they possess to change the way things are done. Reflecting upon their experiences may lead them to alter subsequent actions. It heightens their sense of who they are, and who they can become. It fosters hope, something that has been eroded in many students for whom socioeconomic or minority status has led to social disenfranchisement.

Of course, reflection improves academic learning as it offers a means of practicing basic skills; it enables a deepening of students' understanding of all subject areas; it reveals the interrelatedness of all subjects; and it nurtures higher-order thinking skills and problem-solving capabilities. Finally, the feedback and analysis made possible through reflection can result in an improved program, as changes are made along the way in concert with ideas generated by brainstorming, developing new strategies, and thinking of new ways to do things. A useful "how-to" guide for reflection can be found at http://www.learningtogive.org/doc/how2guide.doc.

Under the previously listed "Reflection Activities" for "Tracking the Trash," there are many ways for students to think about and process the experience of this recycling activity. They can be asked at the outset for their predictions regarding the effect of the activity on their own beliefs and habits. They can make daily entries in a journal to keep track of their ideas and feelings as the project progresses. They can discuss group dynamics and interpersonal issues that surfaced during the group activity. Group discussions would provide a valuable forum for students to share their experiences and opinions on the project. They can also share ideas after the fact, processing the final presentation and the feelings of accomplishment and achievement as well as any problems or disappointments they experienced. All reflections can be used to inform future projects, and students can brainstorm about what projects they want to take on next.

An area that can be nurtured by reflection is that which feeds the students' development of a moral structure and a system of values that guide actions. Posing ethical dilemmas to students at this age is a powerful and engaging way to place them in situations where they must test their developing morality and values in authentic ways. For example, the following activity "Recycling in the Neighborhood," poses such an ethical dilemma. The essential questions for reflection are "What is the responsibility of a person to the environment?" "Does a person have a moral responsibility to engage others in protecting the environment?" "What are the ethics of environmental protection?" Such questions stimulate caring attitudes as well as the inferential and abstract thinking processes developing in these students, putting the learning in service learning.

Recycling in the Neighborhood

Context

Students are presented with an ethical dilemma specifically derived from their service experience in which children like themselves must make a difficult choice in which personal beliefs regarding environmental protection may conflict with social relationships. The intention is to provide a context that illustrates the complexity of decision-making relative to environmental protection. When students are encouraged to see all sides of an argument, they will be empowered to anticipate roadblocks and other impediments that can arise in the process of effecting social reform of all kinds.

Objectives

1. Students will be aware of the consequences resulting from each person's decision to recycle or not to recycle paint and motor oil. They will be able to explain the consequences of the illegal disposal of these materials. This supports Standard 5 of the Science and Technology frameworks, which specify that students explain the elements of a system: goals, inputs, processes, outputs, and feedback (Massachusetts Department of Education, 2001b).

2. Students will also be able to provide at least three reasons why some people do not always follow the law regarding hazardous waste disposal. The students' explanation will demonstrate a sense of their appreciation of the complexity of decision-making involving the environment. They will be able to articulate the ethical dilemma, and infer and explain the perspectives of people with differing views. This activity is supportive of Standard 11 of the language arts curriculum on Reading and Literature, focusing on Theme, which addresses the analysis and evaluation of themes, distinguishing theme from topic. In this activity, the theme of perspective is explored, as opposed to the topic of service (Massachusetts Department of Education, 2001a).

3. Students will be able to explain a decision made by consensus and to provide at least three reasons why it is a good way to make decisions and three reasons why it is a poor way to make decisions. This objective supports

Standard 13 of the English Language Arts frameworks (Massachusetts Department of Education, 2001a), which specifies that students analyze and use evidence in making an argument, and also Mental Health Standard 5 whereby students are asked to explain a model for decision-making that includes gathering information, predicting outcomes, identifying moral implications, and evaluating outcomes (Massachusetts Department of Education, 1999).

4. Students will apply communication skills to foster a better social environment to the meet Interpersonal Relationship Standard 7 of the curriculum frameworks (Massachusetts Department of Education, 1999).

Procedure

1. Students are divided into groups of four or five.
2. Each student in each group is given the story "Recycling in the Neighborhood" (as shown below) and reads it.
3. Each student in each group is given a set of questions for discussion in each group.
4. They discuss the questions.
5. Each group does a role-play within its own group, with each member assuming the role of a character from the story. One person is Sarah, another is the first neighbor, and another the second neighbor. If there are five in the group, third and fourth members play an angel and a devil. The angel exhorts Sarah to talk to the neighbors about recycling; the devil tells her to mind her own business and lets others do the same. Sarah talks to both of them, giving her reasons for talking about it or for ignoring it. Group members then switch roles until each has a chance to be every character.
6. Each group must then arrive at a consensus decision regarding Sarah's next step.
7. Each group designates a member to present their response to the class. Group members can field questions from the class about how they reached the decision and explain if anyone in the group dissented.
8. Each member of the class is given the set of reflection questions that follow to answer individually on paper.

Ethical Dilemma

Recycling in the Neighborhood

Sarah is an 11-year-old sixth grader at Anytown Middle School. Recently, she participated in a recycling service-learning project in her class. Part of the service project involved letting people in the community know about the need to recycle. The students also studied Anytown's laws regarding the disposal of paint, motor oil, and other harmful substances. They produced flyers to remind their parents and neighbors that if they place such toxic items in the trash, they could end up in the landfill where they could adversely affect the water supply. They explained that the proper thing to do was to bring used motor oil back to the place where it was purchased and to take old cans of paint to a recycling facility where those materials would be taken care of properly. The students contacted Anytown's mayor and learned that the town could not afford to include disposal of toxic waste in the regular town recycling program, and that people have to pay for those services themselves.

As Sarah walked home from school that day, her retired neighbor and former kindergarten teacher Mrs. Smith was untying a bag of trash she had put out earlier. As Sarah came by, she said "Oh hi Sarah! How was your day? I've been painting all morning and just realized it was trash day, so I'm sticking these cans in here. I can't afford to pay someone else to get rid of them. I pay enough for town services as it is! Oh, but here I am rambling on ... sorry dear ... how was school? What are they teaching you these days?" "Oh just the usual!" said Sarah, and added, "I have to get home. We have a new puppy and I'm supposed to take him out right after school! Bye!" "Ok dear, see you later," replied Mrs. Smith, as she added the paint cans to her trash and tied the bag up again.

Sarah went home and immediately returned to the sidewalk with her new puppy, "Green," on a leash. Green was very excited and pulled her along, as he sniffed at the trash bags of her other neighbor, Mr. White. Green was most interested in one bag, and lunged at it, tearing at with his teeth and shaking his head. "Green, stop it!" commanded Sarah, but it was too late. The contents of the bag were all over the sidewalk. Sarah was surprised to see several dusty bottles of motor oil among a great deal of meat scraps, which Green was now lunging at, while Sarah held him back. Just then, Mr. White came out, asking what all the fuss was about. Sarah explained about Green. Mr. White said "Green? You are calling him Green? That's unusual. I've never heard of a dog named Green. Do you think he looks green?" "No" laughed Sarah, "I called him that because we're studying recycling in school and we're learning how to keep things green. I think it's really cool, so I named my puppy Green." "Well, I guess that makes sense, and recycling is a good idea, but I'd like to know who has the time? I know I don't! That's why I'm just throwing this old motor oil out in the trash. I don't have time to take it back to the store! Who does? Anyway, not your problem, kid. Have a good day, and have fun with Green." "Ok Mr. White. See you later," said Sarah.

As she continued to walk Green, Sarah wondered if she should go back to both neighbors and tell them about recycling and point out how what they were doing was wrong. Both neighbors were friends of the family, and one was her former teacher. But Sarah firmly believed in recycling and could see that their actions could affect people's health for years to come. What should she do?

Students will answer the following reflection questions:

1. How and why should Sarah tell the neighbors to dispose of the motor oil and paint?
2. How and why should Sarah not say anything further about recycling to the neighbors?

3. Summarize the ethical dilemma and explain your group's decision.
4. Tell why you do or do not agree with the group decision.
5. Should decisions be made by consensus? Why or why not?

Promoting Resiliency

School psychologists and school counselors have long recognized the importance of resiliency for positive developmental outcomes, and researchers indicate that schools can be powerful in their ability to foster resiliency. Some of the key characteristics of schools that have been successful in fostering resiliency in students include the establishment and enforcement of clear boundaries and expectations, high expectations of success, encouragement of goal setting and mastery, and opportunities to participate in meaningful activities that can include leadership and decision-making experience (Henderson & Milstein, 2002). Service learning incorporates all of these factors that in turn promote resiliency.

In addition, this service-learning curriculum nurtures resiliency by recognizing and rewarding multiple learning styles and the multiple intelligences proposed by educational psychologist Howard Gardner (1993). Certainly, its focus on the environment taps Gardner's "naturalist" realm of intelligence. Verbal/linguistic intelligence is utilized when students interview the cafeteria manager and communicate their findings at the school assembly; logical/mathematical intelligence is tapped through analysis of trash data. Students use their interpersonal intelligence when working together in groups, and reflection activities stimulate intrapersonal intelligence. The activity also offers students an opportunity to use their bodily kinesthetic intelligence through the exercise of gross and fine motor skills, for example, in collecting trash items and graphing data. The kinesthetic and naturalist intelligences have been cited as areas of particular value in reaching many of the "at-risk" students typically referred to school psychologists and counselors (Shepard, 2004). Finally, students could sing or compose songs about recycling, using their musical/rhythmic intelligence. Thus, the multi-faceted nature of the service-learning project gives students multiple opportunities to experience success, and therefore to realize self-efficacy.

Links to the Developmental Assets

Developmental assets are experiences and qualities of life that contribute toward the outcome of young people who are healthy, caring, and responsible (Search Institute, 2000). The middle school service-learning activity helps to build those developmental assets in an authentic context that provides many "teachable" moments for incidental social–emotional learning.

As students work together, recording the information on lunch throwaways each day, they are building relationships and not merely collecting data. They are learning how to work with both peers and adults, as they perform the activity with their classmates and they are required to interview the cafeteria manager, as well as present their results to adults from the community and faculty members of the school. Out of necessity, they will need to negotiate and resolve conflicts. Over the course of the activity, the students are becoming experts in the field of recycling in the school. They are researching what can and cannot be recycled; they are learning how much food is regularly thrown away. They are discovering what governmental guidelines are in place, affecting the use and disposal of foods in the school. In short, they are becoming valuable resources of knowledge on the subject.

The supervision and preparation teachers and staff offer students in carrying out this activity make them feel safe. Moreover, because the students are aware of acceptable versus unacceptable behavior during the activity, they understand what is expected of them. Boundaries are made clear and expectations are set high, fostering self-control and achievement motivation.

It is likely that many students, prior to participating in this activity, never gave a second thought to what they threw in the trash. By linking the information learned in the classroom to their "real lives" in the cafeteria, students can learn that their education can be applied to solve issues and problems affecting their world and, as they reflect on their new knowledge and experiences, their worldview may change, and thereby their behavior. They may raise the level of environmental awareness in their homes, as well as within the school, in turn affecting the community at large. Having experienced such changes and growth in their personal outlook, young people may be inspired to a greater commitment to learning about other issues.

The reflection phase of the activity helps young people to identify and internalize their values. Through education on an issue such as recycling, they are able to develop values that are based on sound evidence as well as considerable thought about a person's responsibility to the environment. Realizing the effect of the choices each person makes on a daily basis in regard to environmental issues on the climate of the entire world is a very powerful thought. Recycling and educating the community about environmental preservation is a way that students in this activity can put their values to work in the real world, and it supports the development of a sense of purpose.

Because the bulk of this service-learning activity is performed as a group, students' social competence is nurtured. They must plan, organize, make decisions, manage conflicts, and take on different roles during the course of the activity. During reflection discussions, they must be respectful listeners to the ideas of others with whom they may not agree. In addition, they must interact positively with teachers and staff.

At the conclusion of this service-learning activity, students will come away with a more positive view of themselves. Their ability to learn about recycling, to investigate the status of trash in the cafeteria, and make recommendations that will inform a school-wide recycling program enables students to see themselves as agents of "real life" social change. This gives them a sense of their own purpose and power.

Modifying the Service Activity for Students with Disabilities

Consonant with the educational philosophies of NASP and ASCA, this service-learning curriculum assumes that *all* students can become competent thinkers, problem solvers, and can make valuable contributions to the community. This means placing students with disabilities in the role of "server" rather than as the recipient of service from others. By assuming a service role, students with disabilities will see themselves as helpers who make valuable contributions to the community. Moreover, the participation of students with disabilities in service projects will provide the community with opportunities to look beyond the disabilities to see their abilities. By grouping the students with disabilities together with their nondisabled peers, walls of fear and ignorance can be broken down between both groups.

Service learning is naturally geared toward addressing the diverse needs of students with disabilities. One reason is that it places students in roles different than what they traditionally take on in school. For example, while the traditional model of education in the United States relies heavily on the use of verbal skills, students within a service-learning curriculum can succeed, even if they are not fluent in the English language, even if abuse and neglect have left them traumatized and without the words to express their experiences, and even if they are merely uncomfortable talking. There are many ways in which students can succeed in service learning without relying on verbal or linguistic skills.

Again, the sixth-grade recycling service-learning activity is an example. The following chart shows how to modify the activity; it provides tips on how to accomplish this; and it lists people you may want to consult or collaborate with in carrying out the activity.

How to Modify the Service Activity for Middle School Grade 6 Students with Disabilities

Disability	Modified Service	Tips	Consult or collaborate with:
Learning disability	Contributes to class report data orally; Include as member of the oral presentation team to school assembly; Make an audiotape of reflections; Ask the student to think of ways in which the information the class collects can be used to change the way things are done in the cafeteria and at home –emphasize "real world" connections	Include visuals of items on data recording chart; Multi-modal instruction; Ask student to explain back what is to be done; Partner with appropriate peer; Minimize written output; Oral assessments; Give verbal praise	Special education inclusion or learning center teachers – provide them with data from the project and use to monitor student progress weekly as students apply data to achieve math and language arts standards; Speech/language pathologist to target areas of weakness

Cognitive impairment	Collect a specific item (such as cans) from each table; Distributing data collection sheets to classmates; Draw pictures for recycling posters for hallways; Include as member of the oral presentation team to school assembly	Provide pre-service instruction, including role-playing; Instruct child-specific aides (if any) on expectations for this activity; Pair with appropriate peer; Work in short blocks of time; Give verbal praise	Life Skills or Applied Behavior Analysis (ABA) teacher; Speech/language pathologist; Occupational therapist; Physical therapist
Attention Deficit Hyperactivity Disorder (ADHD)	Change roles daily (one day collect bottles, the next collect unused milk); Emphasize hands-on, active duties; minimize inactive tasks, such as writing; Allow oral reflection; Have student tutor others about recycling	Allow frequent breaks with alternate planned activity; Structure time and supervise closely; Provide written checklist of duties; Group with appropriate peers; Position front and center; Link to behavior plan	Classroom or special education teachers for information on behavior management and plans
Asperger Syndrome Nonverbal Learning Disability (NVLD)	Let student choose and research an area of interest in recycling and use information to inform school-wide report; Let student work with the same group of students each day; Let student teach classmates about area of interest – tap into cognitive strengths, facilitate leadership position; Emphasize reflection on how the project will affect others	Role-play activities before service; Group with appropriate peer; Monitor service activities; Facilitate group discussions; Review and process social interactions of service in small group; Explain service in relation to the "big picture"	Speech/language pathologist for social pragmatic work; Classroom or special education teachers for math manipulatives that facilitate student learning; monitor progress toward achievement of math goals weekly, using weekly data from project
Emotional or Behavioral Disability	Work within a small group of appropriate peers; Allow student to choose their role in the activity; Offer the opportunity to do individualized project,	Structure and supervise closely; Communicate successes to assistant principal and home;	ABA teacher, classroom or special education teachers; Child-specific aide;

(Continued)

(Continued)

Disability	Modified Service	Tips	Consult or collaborate with:
	such as creating something from discarded items; Offer leadership position within small group; Include student in group that presents results in assembly	Give verbal praise; Link to behavioral plan at school and home; Offer frequent breaks	Assistant principal; Parent/guardian
Physical or health impairment	Modify physical participation or reduce time spent in activities, according to individual needs	Ensure accessibility for those with mobility impairments; Consider a fixed location, reduce physical activities	Child-specific aide to learn of special needs; Other specialists according to particular student situation; Parent/guardian
Sensory impairment: Blindness	Let student tape input to class report; Encourage student to advocate need for Braille labels for recycling bins to administration	Determine need for Braille; Pair with a buddy; Position out of high-traffic zones, clear away obstructions; Investigate food allergies and take appropriate precautions	Child-specific aide; Classroom or special education teachers; Vision or mobility specialist Parent/guardian
Sensory impairment: Deafness	Modify assessments as needed; Allow student to work individually to research information on recycling if cafeteria noise is too confusing; Encourage student to present information at assembly with sign language interpreter if feasible	Pair with a buddy to assist in following oral directions; Accompany directions with signs; Develop safety provisions and emergency signals; Always secure student's attention before presenting information; Do not turn away from student when presenting information	Child-specific aide; Classroom or special education teachers; Speech/language pathologist; Sign language interpreter; Parent/Guardian

In modifying the activity for students with disabilities, we take the strength-based, solution-focused approach recognized by many in the counseling field as optimal for use in the school setting (Kahn, 2000; Metcalf, 1995; Sklare, 2005) and compatible with the paradigm shift in school psychology and school counseling from problem identification to problem solution (Reschly & Yessldyke, 2002; Stone & Dahir, 2006). How does the service activity relate to counseling? The idea behind this is to use the service-learning experience as an alternative authentic intervention to achieve the same social and emotional learning goals set forth for students to achieve through counseling. It is a different path toward the same end, but carries the added benefit of support for academic learning and career development.

The notion behind solution-focused counseling is to direct attention to what is working and away from what is not working; to focus on strengths rather than deficits. Solution-focused approaches de-emphasize diagnoses, are future-oriented, and place the counselor in the role of a facilitator, or coach, as opposed to an expert (Kahn, 2000). That is why, when activities are modified, the emphasis is on the student's strengths rather than on areas in which they struggle.

School psychologists or school counselors in a middle school could work with an individual student or a small group on this recycling service project, work on the project in conjunction with the general education class, or work in collaboration with other specialists. Consider a social skills group that includes a student with Asperger syndrome, a student with attention deficit hyperactivity disorder (ADHD), a student who has a mild cognitive impairment, and a student with a specific learning disability. In addition, there could be a student who has a poor attitude toward school and lack of engagement in academics, coupled with truant behavior, defiance of authority, and disrespect of staff; nevertheless, among students, he is considered to be "cool" and a leader. A social skills "lunch bunch" group might meet once a week in the counselor's office to talk. The students seem to interact well in the small group, but the teacher reports that the students are still experiencing interpersonal difficulties in the "real world" of the classroom. As an alternative to this small social skills group, the students could be assigned to the service-learning recycling project "Tracking the Trash." Each group member would require certain modifications in the activity to meet their unique learning needs. Because service-learning projects are multifaceted, there are multiple ways in which to arrange tasks to capitalize on the students' strengths and to accommodate their special needs.

Student with Learning Disabilities

Assume the first student is a girl with a specific learning disability who has particular difficulty with written expression. In view of this difficulty, it is advisable to enable her to communicate in a different way. For example, she could contribute to data collection and class recommendations orally, make an audiotape of her reflections, and interview others for their thoughts on changes the cafeteria could make to its food disposal system. In collecting data from the cafeteria, provide the student with learning disabilities a list of the items to be counted, including a visual of each category. Give directions both visually and verbally and ask the student to explain back to you what is to be done, to check for understanding. Try to group her with an appropriate peer who can provide assistance when needed. Minimize the written output expected from her, and consider oral assessments. As with all students, her service efforts need to be recognized. Consult the special education inclusion or learning center teacher for specifics on academic areas the student needs to address. The speech/language pathologist would also be a natural choice for you to engage in a collaborative effort. Provide them with data from the project and use their input to monitor student progress weekly. Social and emotional goals to increase self-esteem and encourage social interactions could be realized through the service-learning project.

Student with Cognitive Impairments

Modification of the service for a girl who has mild cognitive impairment might involve asking her to collect a specific item from each lunch table, such as aluminum cans. She could also be put in charge of distributing data collection sheets to classmates; she could draw pictures for posters promoting recycling to be hung in the hallways; and she could be included as a member of the oral presentation team at the school assembly. Tips on helping this student with these tasks would include providing preservice instruction through role-plays, and allowing her to work in short blocks of time. Pair her with an appropriate peer and offer frequent verbal praise as she works. Instruct her classroom aide(s), if any, on expectations for this activity. It would also be advisable to consult or work in conjunction with the Life Skills or Applied Behavior Analysis (ABA) teacher, the speech/language pathologist, the occupational therapist, and the physical therapist in order to learn more about the student's needs and get specifics on how to modify the service-learning project for the best outcome. Goals to promote social interaction, work habits, and managing frustration would be incorporated in the service-learning plans.

Student with ADHD

Accommodations for a boy who is diagnosed with ADHD might include allowing him to change his task assignments frequently. For example, one day he could count bottles, the next he could collect unused milk. Emphasize hands-on, active duties for him, such as physically collecting items and helping to discard them when classmates have recorded the data. If there are any props or visuals to be set up for the school-wide assembly where the class will present its findings and make recommendations for a cafeteria recycling program, ask this student to be in charge of that. Minimize sedentary duties, such as data recording, and written tasks. Allow him to record his reflections on tape. Allow frequent breaks and design an alternative activity just in case your initial plans have to be changed. For example, he might enjoy tutoring younger students about recycling. Structure his time and supervise him closely; provide a written checklist of duties. Group him with an appropriate peer. Position him front and center in the activity, and link his behavior in the service activity to a daily behavior management plan with specific goals and reinforcement for appropriate behavior. Consult classroom and special education teachers in regard to such a plan.

Student with Asperger Syndrome

A modification for a boy diagnosed with Asperger Syndrome would be to allow him to choose an area of his interest in recycling, ask him to research it, and use the information to inform the school-wide recommendations. Let this student work with the same group of students each day, and encourage him to share his area of interest with his classmates through a personal oral presentation or other means of his choice. Capitalize on his cognitive strength in the verbal realm. Ask him to be a spokesperson for his group in class discussions; encourage his input to written recommendations to the school. In reflection activities, ask him how he feels the project will affect others in the school and the community. This student's activities in group situations should be monitored so that social interactions can be facilitated. It is advisable to review and process social interactions that take place in the actual service activity in a small group setting as well. In addition, it would be helpful to explain the service activity to this student as it relates to the "big picture" of environmental concerns. Consult the classroom or special education teacher for advice on the use of math manipulatives that might enhance the student's learning. Monitor weekly progress toward achievement of math goals, using weekly data from the project.

Student with Behavior Problems

The service activity could be modified for a student with behavioral issues. Key findings from the research on the use of service learning for students with emotional/behavioral disorders suggest that academic and affective learning outcomes expand the more closely connected the service is to the core curriculum and with the amount of time a student spends in the experience and in reflecting upon it. Second, the quality of the learning and ability to apply the knowledge gained is greatly influenced by the extent to which the student is given responsibility and tasks of significance to perform (Muscott, 2000).

In this example, the student has shown leadership qualities among his peers (although they have been used in a negative direction) with a goal of garnering attention. Put him in a leadership role in the service activity. Ask him to be a team leader, in charge of data collection at several tables. Convey confidence in his ability to carry out his duties well. Also consider offering him the chance to do something special. For example, ask him to take an interest of his and apply it to the project. If he plays the guitar, ask him to make up a song about recycling. If he likes artwork, ask him to make a sculpture out of discarded items. Display his creation in the school lobby. Give him significant responsibilities. Focus on his capabilities and show him that the school values his contributions. It is also important to communicate the successes of this student to the assistant principal and to his caregivers, and ask them to give positive feedback to the student. Link his activities to a behavioral management plan. Give verbal praise and recognition of his efforts to reinforce positive roles. Consult with classroom teachers and the assistant principal regarding disciplinary records and his parents or guardians to learn more about home issues that might affect him at school, and to encourage a relationship between his caregivers and the school.

These examples are just a few ways that the service activity could be modified for students with particular disabilities. Additional suggestions are provided in the charts within the "Pre-K-12 Service-Learning Blueprints" at the end of this section.

Consultation and Collaboration with Others

Anyone familiar with an Individual Educational Plan (IEP) can see that responsibility for achieving student goals and objectives is often shared by multiple staff members. Often, the IEP lists a number of services rendered by a number of specialists. Consider the case of a student diagnosed with Asperger syndrome. The student may meet with the school psychologist or school counselor to address social or emotional issues, the speech/language pathologist for pragmatics of communication, and the occupational therapist to address repetitive motor mannerisms. Many of the specialist areas overlap in regard to the goals of their interventions. In such cases, it makes sense to consult colleagues to learn about how they are approaching the intervention goals and to see if the service-learning activity might offer a means of collaboration.

In the case of the middle school service-learning activity, the specialists could collaborate within the context of the service activity. For example, the school psychologist or counselor and the speech/language pathologist could alternate periods of time directing and facilitating the social interactions of the student within a small group working on the activity, since there is a mutual goal of improving social skills. The occupational therapist could work with the student as he or she collects cafeteria refuse, perhaps giving the student a particular type of writing instrument to facilitate his or her grip in recording data. By blending roles, sharing ideas, and working together with colleagues in a common context, the likelihood of reaching mutual goals is increased. If everyone is "on the same page" in terms of a consistent and meaningful context for intervention with the student, then there is an increased probability of generalization beyond the service activity to other "real" situations.

Response to Intervention Perspectives

The service-learning project not only supports social, emotional, and academic learning, it can be used to confirm student progress or reveal shortcomings in those areas. In the Response to Intervention (RtI) model, service-learning programs can be used at the Tier 1 level, as a core intervention for all students, in a preventive, proactive approach. Service learning can also apply to Tier 2 as a targeted group intervention for at-risk students, and at the Tier 3 level as a service-learning intervention for individual students. In the case of the "Tracking the Trash" activity, teachers could apply it to the entire class in a Tier 1 application, or school psychologists and counselors could independently or with other specialists implement service-learning as an intervention at the Tier 2 or 3 level for students who require more intensive social, emotional, or academic interventions.

Response to Intervention data also can be used as evidence of the effectiveness of school-based mental health services. In addition to collecting data about an individual student's response to a service-learning intervention, group data can be collected and disaggregated, separating ethnicity, gender, or socioeconomic status, to reveal systemic issues. This broader view would enable school psychologists and school counselors to identify critical elements in the achievement gap, and to communicate issues to administrators and faculty. Data should be collected prior to the start of the service-learning program, during its active phase, and at its conclusion. School-based mental health professionals can use data from the program to demonstrate its effectiveness to administration, faculty, and school committees, representing a departure from the qualitative assessments often used to evaluate service-learning programs. According to Muscott (2000), with few exceptions, anecdotal evidence has dominated the methodology in assessing service-learning programs for children with emotional or behavioral disabilities.

Data for Professional Accountability

Quantifiable outcomes are also a powerful alternative to more traditional forms of accountability used by school counselors, such as the number of counseling sessions held with students, or the number of classroom presentations made, both of which have little connection with the academic mission. Conversely, data demonstrating gains in academic performance, discipline referral reductions, or increased school attendance are compelling ways to demonstrate the positive impact of school psychological or counseling services as key to students' academic success (Dahir & Stone, 2003).

Lighting the Fire

Although a district-wide service-learning program would be ideal, Rome was not built in a day, and service learning is more likely to start as a small grassroots effort, one classroom, one group, or one student at a time. This is likely to be the best way to begin. Change is difficult anywhere, but perhaps particularly so in a school, where time is tight and there is pressure to achieve standards. Additional mandates handed down from administrators are unlikely to be readily or cheerfully adopted. Also, reluctance on the part of staff to try new things may pose a barrier. Teachers and staff may not initially realize that service learning would make it easier for them to achieve their goals, rather than being an additional burden. As poet W. B. Yeats said, "Education is not the filling of a pail, but the lighting of a fire." For example, perhaps you start by involving a group of students in service learning during their regularly scheduled counseling session. The students are enthused and tell their friends. Other counselors in the building hear about it and want to try it too. Perhaps a teacher has expressed an interest in involving students in a service-learning activity. In the role of classroom consultants, school psychologists and counselors could offer teachers advice about integrating service with the curriculum, addressing social, emotional, career, and academic goals, and accommodating students with special needs. Other teachers hear of these projects and want to try it in their classrooms. And so it goes. A small spark is all that may be needed to ignite the flame for service learning.

Pre-K-12 Service-Learning Blueprints

The following pages contain blueprints for service-learning projects spanning pre-K-12 education. Illustrative examples are provided for pre-K and grades 3, 6, and 10. Each example offers an environmental service-learning project idea, connections to curriculum standards, ideas for reflection, and modifications for students with special needs.

Blueprint

Preschool General Education Classroom Activity: "From Trash to Treasures"

Tasks

Students are shown pictures of a landfill and given an explanation of how trash is piled up and will eventually fill the landfill. The class discusses ways to reduce the amount of trash and explores ideas on ways in which materials such as boxes, paper, and cardboard might be reused. Students' families and the school community contribute discarded items. The children think of things to make from them, considering colors, shapes, and textures. Possibilities include bookmarks, collages, sculptures, storage containers, picture frames, or wheelbarrow flower pots made from old laundry detergent scoops. Students count and sort recycled materials as they are collected. They will create new objects from recycled materials for use as artwork for the school to promote recycling and donate appropriate handmade gifts to nursing homes in the community. Finally, they create puppets and other props for a puppet show they will create to tell the story of their recycling project at a school assembly for other students, faculty, and caregivers.

Essential Questions Posed to Promote Social/Emotional Growth

- What does it mean to throw something "away"?
- How can we reduce the amount of trash sent to the landfill?

- Why should the community care about recycling?
- What did you like best about the project? What did you not like? Why?
- What did you like best about working with your group? What did you not like? Why?

Links to the Curriculum Standards

This activity is designed to help students' achieve the following curriculum standards set forth by the Massachusetts Department of Education: (Note: The list is not exhaustive, but representative in nature.)

DOE Curriculum Standard	Description
English Language Arts Standard 2 for Questioning, Listening, and Contributing	contribute knowledge to class discussion to develop topic for class project
English Language Arts Standard 4 for Vocabulary and Concept Development	identify and sort common words into various classifications
Math Standard 1 for Number Sense and Operations	count by ones to at least 20
Math Standard 4 for Number Sense and Operations	compare sets of up to at least 10 concrete objects using appropriate language (e.g., none, fewer than, same number of, one more than) and order numbers
Mental Health Standard 5 for Identity Development	**identify feelings**
Mental Health Standard 7 for Interpersonal Relationships	**describe good friendships**

Reflection Activities:

- Preservice discussion on what happens to things once we are finished with them
- Drawings of feelings about the project
- Puppet show depicting project and outcomes
- Oral reflections on gifts created for others
- Discussions about working together

Services Provided:

- Provide school and community with recycled items
- Reduce amount of trash
- Raise community awareness of the need for recycling
- Gifts for seniors

Service Learning:

- Awareness that each person has an effect on the environment
- Creative thinking—how to use things in different ways
- Experience of giving to others
- Acquisition of language arts and math skills

Career Connections:

- Artist
- Designer
- Advertiser/marketer
- Inventor
- Educator
- Engineer
- Public relations representative

Developmental Assets Supported:

- External: Caring school climate; parent involvement in schooling; community values youth; youth as resources; service to others
- Internal: School engagement; bonding to school; caring; responsibility; planning and decision making; self-esteem; sense of purpose

How to Modify the Service Activity for Preschool Students with Disabilities

Disability	Modified Service	Tips	Consult or collaborate with:
Cognitive impairment	Distribute materials to the class; help sort things	Provide pre-service instruction, role-play; instruct child-specific aides (f any) on expectations for this activity; provide verbal praise	Life Skills or Applied Behavior Analysis (ABA) teacher; Speech/language pathologist; Occupational therapist; Physical therapist
Physical or health impairment	Modify physical participation as needed, or reduce time spent	Ensure accessibility for those with mobility impairments; Consider a fixed location, such as cafeteria duties, reduce physical activities	Child-specific aide to learn of special needs; Other specialists according to particular student situation; Parent/guardian
Sensory impairment Blindness	Provide with a cup and two bowls, one with sand or soil and the other empty. Give student	Pair with a buddy; Position out of high-traffic zones, clear away	Child-specific aide; Classroom or special education teachers; Parent/guardian

	layering materials, such as magazine or newspapers. Ask them to pour some sand or dirt into the bowl and add a later of newspaper. Then ask them to keep alternating sand or soil and layering materials to create a miniature landfill. Provide multi-textural materials; Ask if student can identify the objects materials came from	obstructions; supervise use of scissors; Provide Braille labels for markers and other supplies	
Sensory impairment: Deafness	Modify assessments as needed; Allow student to work individually in a quieter area, if possible, if classroom noise is too confusing; Encourage student to present personal observations on the project to the class	Accompany directions with signs; Develop safety provisions and emergency signals; Always secure student's attention before presenting information; Do not turn away from student when presenting information	Child-specific aide; Classroom or special education teachers; Parent/guardian

Blueprint

Elementary Grade Three General Education Classroom Activity: "Creating Community Compost"

Tasks

Students will learn the difference between how wastes are disposed in a landfill as opposed to composting. They will see that the purpose of a landfill is to isolate trash from air and water. They will realize that trash in a landfill does not decompose much. Conversely, students will learn the purpose of composting is to bury wastes in such a way that they decompose quickly, creating a nutrient-rich fertilizer for community gardens. They will learn what a compost pile is and how to create a compost bin. (It can be as simple as a garbage can with holes drilled into it.) Food scraps (with the exception of meat and dairy products) from the cafeteria, and grass and yard clippings from the maintenance staff will comprise the compost pile. Students will estimate and find the area and perimeter of the compost bin and maintain records of compost temperature, organic material added to the pile, the days the pile is turned, and the date compost will be ready. The compost will be available to the community. Students will write letters to caregivers telling them about the project and advocating for recycling at home.

Essential Questions Posed to Promote Social/Emotional Growth

- Why make compost when we have a landfill?
- Why should people work together to solve community problems?
- What does it mean to be wasteful?
- Did your group work well together? Why? If not, what did you do?
- What was fun about the project? What was frustrating?

Links to the Curriculum Standards

This activity is designed to help students' achieve the following curriculum standards set forth by the Massachusetts Department of Education: (Note: The list is not exhaustive, but representative in nature.)

DOE Curriculum Standard	Description
Science and Technology/Engineering Standard 11 for Energy and Living Things	describe how energy derived from the sun is used by plants to produce sugars (photosynthesis) and is transferred within a food chain from producers (plants) to consumers to decomposers
Math Standard 4 for Measurement	estimate and find area and perimeter of irregular shape using diagrams, models, and grids or by measuring
English Language Arts Standard 19 for Writing	write brief summaries of information gathered through research
English Language Arts Standard 24 for Research	identify and apply steps in conducting and reporting research
Health Standard 12 for Consumer Health and Resource Management	name and weigh criteria for selecting a consumer product and evaluate the product's safety and health aspects
Mental Health Standard 5 Emotional Development	**learn skills to manage stress**
Mental Health Standard 7 for Interpersonal Relationships	**define character traits such as honesty and kindness and describe their contribution to interpersonal relationships**

Reflection Activities:

- Preservice reflection through discussion: why do we throw things away?
- What do the students predict will happen to the food scraps in the compost bin?
- Do students think this activity will change their habits? Why or why not?

- Journal entries on ideas of what other things could be recycled
- Group discussions on why we need to recycle; share examples of when someone wasted something, how they felt about it, and what they would do differently now

Services Provided:

- Compost provided for the community
- Amount of solid wastes sent to the landfill by the school reduced through this method of recycling
- Student letters home raise community awareness of need for recycling

Service Learning:

- Awareness of personal habits in regard to generation of waste
- Learning personal responsibility for the environment
- Learning the effect each person has on the environment
- Relationship of personal choices to group outcomes
- Ability to work collaboratively with others
- Appreciation of community
- Authentic application of science, math, and language arts skills

Career Connections:

- Scientist
- Researcher
- Mathematician
- Writer
- Politician
- Public relations representative
- Construction worker
- Educator

Developmental Assets Supported:

- External: Caring school climate; caring neighborhood; community values youth; youth as resources; service to others; high expectations
- Internal: Achievement motivation; school engagement; bonding to school; caring; responsibility; planning and decision-making; personal power; self-esteem; sense of purpose

How to Modify the Service Activity for Grade 3 Elementary School Students with Disabilities

Disability	Modified Service	Tips	Consult or collaborate with:
Learning disability	Contributes to class report data orally; Include as member of the oral presentation team to school assembly; Make an audiotape of reflections; Ask the student to think of how composting can be an ongoing activity at the school and at home – emphasize "real world" connections	Include visuals of items to be collected and avoided; Multi-modal instruction; Ask student to explain back what is to be done; Partner with appropriate peer; Minimize written output; Oral assessments; Give verbal praise	Special education inclusion or learning center teachers – provide them with data from the project and use to monitor student progress weekly as students apply data to achieve math and language arts standards; Speech/language pathologist to target areas of weakness
Cognitive impairment	Distribute data collection sheets to classmates; Draw pictures of composting for posters in hallways	Provide pre-service instruction, including role-playing; Instruct child-specific aides (if any) on expectations for this activity; Pair with appropriate peer; Work in short blocks of time; Give verbal praise	Life Skills or Applied Behavior Analysis (ABA) teacher; Speech/language pathologist; Occupational therapist; Physical therapist
Attention Deficit Hyper-activity Disorder (ADHD)	Change roles daily (one day collect food scraps, the next work on turning the pile); Emphasize hands-on, active duties; minimize inactive tasks, such as recording data; allow oral reflection; Have student tutor younger students about composting	Allow frequent breaks with alternate planned activity; Structure time and supervise closely; Provide color-coded written checklist of duties; Group with appropriate peers; Position front and center; Link to behavior plan	Classroom or special education teachers for information on behavior management and plans
Asperger Syndrome Nonverbal Learning Disability (NVLD)	Let student choose and research an area of interest in composting and present the information to the class; Let student work with the same group of students each day;	Role-play activities before service; Group with appropriate peer; Monitor service activities; Facilitate group discussions;	Speech/language pathologist for social pragmatic work;

	Let student teach classmates about area of interest – tap into cognitive strengths, facilitate leadership position; Emphasize reflection on how the project will affect others	Review and process social interactions of service in small group; Explain service in relation to the "big picture"	Classroom or special education teachers for math manipulatives that facilitate student learning; monitor progress toward achievement of math goals weekly, using weekly data from project
Emotional or Behavioral Disability	Work within a small group of appropriate peers; Allow student to choose their role in the activity; Offer the opportunity to do individualized project, such as growing a bean plant using compost; Offer leadership position within small group	Structure and supervise closely; Communicate successes to assistant principal and home; Give verbal praise; Link to behavioral plan at school and home; Offer frequent breaks	ABA teacher, classroom or special education teachers; Child-specific aide; Assistant principal; Parent/guardian
Physical or health impairment	Modify physical participation or reduce time spent in activities, according to individual needs	Ensure accessibility for those with mobility impairments; Consider a fixed location, such as cafeteria duties, reduce physical activities	Child-specific aide to learn of special needs; Other specialists according to particular student situation; Parent/guardian
Sensory impairment: Blindness	Let student turn the compost by hand (with protective gloves); Encourage student to describe personal observations of the smell of the compost to the class	Pair with a buddy; Position out of high-traffic zones, clear away obstructions; Investigate food allergies and take appropriate precautions	Child-specific aide; Classroom or special education teachers; Parent/guardian
Sensory impairment: Deafness	Modify assessments as needed; Allow student to work individually to research information on composting if cafeteria noise is too confusing; Encourage student to present personal observations of the changing appearance of compost to the class	Accompany directions with signs; Develop safety provisions and emergency signals; Always secure student's attention before presenting information; Do not turn away from student when presenting information; inform cafeteria and maintenance staff of student communication needs	Child-specific aide; Classroom or special education teachers; Parent/guardian

Blueprint

Middle School Grade Six General Education Classroom Activity: "Tracking the Trash"

Tasks

Students will learn how much food is thrown away at their school each day and use the information to educate other students and inform a cafeteria recycling program by:

- recording the number of students at their lunch table, the number of foil, paper, cans, bottles, juice boxes milk cartons, and plastic utensils per student each day for one month,
- asking students to pour any leftover milk into empty gallon containers and record daily amounts,
- totaling each category, as well as determine a ratio of trash items to student on a monthly basis,
- illustrating data on bar graphs and pie charts, and determining mean, mode, median, maximum and minimum, and range for each trash category,
- interviewing the cafeteria manager to learn what foods are thrown away, what happens to leftovers, and what governmental guidelines must be followed in planning and packaging meals,
- presenting findings and making recommendations in a school-wide assembly to fellow students, faculty, and parents.

Essential Questions Posed for Social/Emotional Growth

- What is the responsibility of a person to the environment?
- What are the ethics of environmental protection?
- Does a person have a moral responsibility to engage others in protecting the environment?
- What is the attitude of other students in the school about recycling in the cafeteria?
- How can a more environmentally responsible climate be encouraged at the school?
- How did the group cooperate to solve problems?
- What was fun about the project? What was frustrating?

Links to the Curriculum Standards

This activity is designed to help students' achieve the following curriculum standards set forth by the Massachusetts Department of Education: (Note: The list is not exhaustive, but representative in nature.)

DOE Curriculum Standard	Description
Math Standard 6 for Data Analysis, Statistics, and Probability	describe and compare data sets using median, mean, mode, maximum, minimum, and range; construct line plots and circle graphs
English Language Arts Standard 2 for Questioning, Listening, and Contributing	gather information through interviews
English Language Arts Standard 3 for Oral Presentations	showing appropriate changes in delivery (gestures, vocabulary, pace, visuals) and using language for dramatic effect
English Language Arts Standard 23 for Organizing Ideas in Writing	placement of details, logical order, organizing information
Health Standard 13 for Ecological Health	describe how business and individuals can work together to solve ecological health problems, such as conserving natural resources and decreasing pollution
Science and Technology Standard 5	explain the elements of a system: goals, inputs, processes, outputs, and feedback
English Language Arts Standard 11 for Themes in Reading and Literature	analyze and evaluate themes; distinguish theme from topic
English Language Arts Standard 13	analyze and use evidence in making an argument
Mental Health Standard 5 for Decision-Making	**explain and practice a model for decision-making that includes gathering information, predicting outcomes, identifying moral implications, and evaluating outcomes**
Mental Health Standard 5 for Coping Skills	**explain how skills such as perceiving situations as opportunities, taking action, and exerting control positively influence self-concept**
Mental Health Standard 5 for Identity Development	**describe the effects of leadership skills on the promotion of teamwork**
Mental Health Standard 5 for Emotional Growth	**apply methods to accommodate a variety of feelings in a constructive way**
Interpersonal Relationships Standard 7 for Communication	**apply both verbal and non-verbal communication skills to develop positive relationships and improve the social environment of the school**

Reflection Activities:

- Preservice reflection through discussion: what do students predict as an outcome? Do they think this activity will change their own beliefs and habits? Why or why not?
- Daily journal entries on use of disposable versus reusable containers and recording of changes in thought and habits
- Daily group discussion of teamwork and interpersonal problems encountered
- Explore ethical dilemmas
- Group discussion following final presentation of results (processing and conclusions); ideas for future projects

Services Provided:

- Education of students in environmentally responsible behavior
- Production of data to inform a school cafeteria recycling program
- Reduction of trash sent to landfill

Service Learning:

- Increasing awareness of personal habits in regard to generation of waste
- Learning personal responsibility for the environment
- Understanding the effect each person has on the environment
- Seeing the relationship of personal choices to group outcomes
- Participating in collaborative problem solving and teamwork
- Appreciating community
- Applying academic skills in an authentic context

Career Connections:

- Reporter
- Researcher
- Mathematician
- Writer
- Politician
- Marketing/public relations representative
- Financial analyst
- Coach
- Educator

Developmental Assets Supported:

- External: Caring school climate; youth as resources; service to others; high expectations
- Internal: Achievement motivation; school engagement; bonding to school; caring; responsibility; planning and decision making; personal power; self-esteem; sense of purpose

How to Modify the Service Activity for Middle School Grade 6 Students with Disabilities

Disability	Modified Service	Tips	Consult or collaborate with:
Learning disability	Contributes to class report data orally; Include as member of the oral presentation team to school assembly; Make an audiotape of reflections; Ask the student to think of ways in which the information the class collects can be used to change the way things are done in the cafeteria and at home – emphasize "real world" connections	Include visuals of items on data recording chart; Multi-modal instruction; Ask student to explain back what is to be done; Partner with appropriate peer; Minimize written output; Oral assessments; Give verbal praise	Special education inclusion or learning center teachers – provide them with data from the project and use to monitor student progress weekly as students apply data to achieve math and language arts standards Speech/language pathologist to target areas of weakness
Cognitive impairment	Collect a specific item (such as cans) from each table; Distributing data collection sheets to classmates; Draw pictures for recycling posters for hallways; Include as member of the oral presentation team to school assembly	Provide pre-service instruction, including role-playing; Instruct child-specific aides (if any) on expectations for this activity; Pair with appropriate peer; Work in short blocks of time; Give verbal praise	Life Skills or Applied Behavior Analysis (ABA) teacher; Speech/language pathologist; Occupational therapist; Physical therapist
Attention Deficit Hyperactivity Disorder (ADHD)	Change roles daily (one day collect bottles, the next collect unused milk); Emphasize hands-on, active duties; minimize inactive tasks, such as writing; Allow oral reflection; Have student tutor others about recycling	Allow frequent breaks with alternate planned activity; Structure time and supervise closely; Provide written checklist of duties; Group with appropriate peers; Position front and center; Link to behavior plan	Classroom or special education teachers for information on behavior management and plans
Asperger Syndrome Nonverbal Learning	Let student choose and research an area of interest in recycling and use	Role-play activities before service; Group with appropriate peer;	Speech/language pathologist for social pragmatic work;

(Continued)

(Continued)

Disability	Modified Service	Tips	Consult or collaborate with:
Disability (NVLD)	information to inform school-wide report; Let student work with the same group of students each day; Let student teach classmates about area of interest – tap into cognitive strengths, facilitate leadership position; Emphasize reflection on how the project will affect others	Monitor service activities; Facilitate group discussions; Review and process social interactions of service in small group; Explain service in relation to the "big picture"	Classroom or special education teachers for math manipulatives that facilitate student learning; monitor progress toward achievement of math goals weekly, using weekly data from project
Emotional or Behavioral Disability	Work within a small group of appropriate peers; Allow student to choose their role in the activity; Offer leadership position within small group; Include student in group that presents results in assembly	Structure and supervise closely; Communicate successes to assistant principal and home; Give verbal praise;Link to behavioral plan at school and home; Offer frequent breaks	ABA teacher, classroom or special education teachers; Child-specific aide; Assistant principal; Parent/guardian
Physical or health impairment	Modify physical participation or reduce time spent in activities, according to individual needs	Ensure accessibility for those with mobility impairments; Consider a fixed location, reduce physical activities	Child-specific aide to learn of special needs; Other specialists according to particular student situation; Parent/guardian
Sensory impairment: Blindness	Let student tape input to class report; Encourage student to advocate need for Braille labels for recycling bins to administration	Determine need for Braille; Pair with a buddy; Position out of high-traffic zones; clear away obstructions; Investigate food allergies and take appropriate precautions	Child-specific aide; Classroom or special education teachers; Vision or mobility specialist Parent/guardian
Sensory impairment: Deafness	Modify assessments as needed; Allow student to work	Pair with a buddy to assist in following oral directions;	Child-specific aide; Classroom or special education teachers;

	individually to research information on recycling if cafeteria noise is too confusing; Encourage student to present information at assembly with sign language interpreter if feasible	Accompany directions with signs; Develop safety provisions and emergency signals; Always secure student's attention before presenting information; Do not turn away from student when presenting information	Sign language interpreter; Speech/language pathologist; Parent/Guardian

Blueprint

High School Grade 10 General Education Classroom Activity: "Recycled 'Cycles"

Tasks

Students solicit and accept donated bicycles from the community, repair and/or refurbish them using materials at hand, and give them to the needy. Students learn and train others in bicycle maintenance and safety. To inform the community of the bicycle recycling and training service, students create a presentation (powerpoint or video) and present it to community agencies.

Essential Questions Posed to Promote Social/Emotional Growth

- Do people have a moral obligation to help those in society who are in need?
- Should global warming affect our lifestyle?
- Do we have a moral obligation to cut down on the use of fossil fuels for transportation?
- How can a more environmentally responsible climate be encouraged at the school?
- How well did your group work together?
- What did you learn about working in a group?

Links to Curriculum Standards:

DOE Curriculum Standard	Description
Technology/Engineering Standard 1 for Engineering Design	practical problem-solving, research, development, and invention; requires designing, drawing, building, testing, and redesigning

(Continued)

(Continued)

DOE Curriculum Standard	Description
English Language Arts Standard 27 for Media Production	create media presentations that effectively use graphics, images, and/or sound to present a distinctive view on a topic
English Language Arts Standard 3 for Oral Presentations	give formal and informal talks to various audiences and for various purposes using appropriate level of formality and rhetorical devices
Health Standard 2 for Physical Activity and Fitness	apply safe practices, rules, procedures, and sportsmanship etiquette to physical activity settings, including how to anticipate potentially dangerous consequences and outcomes of participation in physical activity
Mental Health Standard 5 for Decision-Making	**identify how decision-making is influenced by sound character**
Mental Health Standard 7 for Interpersonal Relationships	**describe the influence of the larger social group on individual conduct**

Reflection Activities:

- Preservice reflection through discussion: have you ever thrown out an old bicycle? Why? Did you ever think of fixing it? Why not? How easy or hard is it for you to get a new bike? Have you thought of other things you could fix? How did it feel to make something useful again? Do you see yourself differently now? How have you changed? Are the "haves" in society obliged to take care of the "have-nots"? Why or why not?
- Has the project affected your career goals?
- Discussion of utility versus desire for extravagance, discussion of how things are marketed to teens/peer pressure—is it hard to be seen riding a "different" bike?
- How are bikes used in other countries—mainly for recreation or transportation? Discuss differences in US versus foreign use of bikes – what does it say about our values? our society?
- Read and discuss *An Inconvenient Truth* (2006), a book on global warming by former Vice President Al Gore
- Daily group discussion of problems encountered and interpersonal feedback
- Group discussion following final presentation of results (processing and conclusions); ideas for future projects

Services Provided:

- Providing the community with ecologically sound transportation; providing adults and children in need with bicycles; reduction of waste via recycling bicycles and other donated materials
- Training the community in bicycle maintenance and safety

- Making the school community aware of the need for environmentally responsible choices
- Providing partnership with school and community
- Providing female students with nontraditional experiences that could lead to nontraditional career choices (engineering, the sciences)

Service Learning:

- Awareness of personal habits in regard to generation of waste
- Experiencing the ability to make a difference for others (empowerment)
- Career preparation: acquisition of job skills; technical know-how, use of tools, planning, cooperation, sharing of resources, group problem solving, responsibility, self-confidence, and taking pride in one's work
- Experience of success in school
- Authentic application of engineering, language arts, fitness and safety knowledge, and media skills

Career Connections:

- Inventor
- Engineer
- Designer
- Politician
- Writer
- Business manager
- Lobbyist
- Coach
- Educator
- Media Specialist

Developmental Assets Supported:

- External: Community values youth; positive peer influence; caring school climate; youth as resources; service to others; high expectations; creative activities
- Internal: Achievement motivation; school engagement; bonding to school; caring; equity and social justice; responsibility; planning and decision making; interpersonal competence; cultural competence; resistance skills; peaceful conflict resolution; personal power; self-esteem

How to Modify the Service Activity for Grade 10 High School Students with Disabilities

Disability	Modified Service	Tips	Consult or collaborate with:
Learning disability	Depending on disability area, emphasize involvement in media	Include visuals of parts and tools to be collected and	Special education inclusion or learning center teachers –

(Continued)

(*Continued*)

Disability	Modified Service	Tips	Consult or collaborate with:
	presentation or in hands-on construction activities; Could be oral spokesperson in media presentation; Make an audiotape of reflections; Ask the student to think of how recycled materials can answer other community needs (ex. grocery carts for elderly) – emphasize "real world" connections; Seek student input to designs	used; Multi-modal instruction; Ask student to explain back what is to be done; Partner with appropriate peer; Minimize written output; Oral assessments; Give verbal praise	provide them with data from the project and use to monitor student progress weekly as students apply data to achieve technology/ engineering and language arts standards; Speech/language pathologist to target areas of weakness
Cognitive impairment	Distribute tools and parts to classmates; Obtain parts and tools as needed during class time; Seek student input to designs	Provide pre-service instruction, including role-playing; Instruct child-specific aides (if any) on expectations for this activity; Pair with appropriate peer; Work in short blocks of time; Give verbal praise	Life Skills or Applied Behavior Analysis (ABA) teacher; Speech/language pathologist; Physical therapist
Attention Deficit Hyperac-tivity Disorder (ADHD)	Give most active roles – gathering equipment; change roles frequently (one day work on one bike, next time on another);Emphasize hands-on, active duties; minimize inactive tasks, such as recording data; allow oral reflection; Have student train others about bicycle maintenance and safety; Seek student input to designs	Allow frequent breaks with alternate planned activity; Structure time and supervise closely; Provide color-coded written checklist of duties; Group with appropriate peers; Position front and center; Link to behavior plan	Classroom or special education teachers for information on behavior management and plans
Asperger Syndrome Nonverbal Learning Disability (NVLD)	Let student choose and research an area of interest in bicycling and present the information to the class; Let student work	Role-play activities before service; Group with appropriate peer; Monitor service activities; Facilitate group discussions;	Speech/language pathologist for social pragmatic work; Classroom or special education teachers for specific

	with the same group of students each day; Let student teach classmates about area of interest – tap into cognitive strengths, facilitate leadership position; Emphasize reflection on how the project will affect others	Review and process social interactions of service in small group; Explain service in relation to the "big picture"	academic goals; monitor progress toward achievement of goals weekly, using weekly data from project
Emotional or Behavioral Disability	Work within a small group of appropriate peers; Allow student to choose their role in the activity; Offer the opportunity to do individualized project, such as designing a very unique bike – provide student background information on bike recipient's needs – ask how would you fill those needs?; Offer leadership position within small group; offer training position to nurture self-image as positive role model; Allow student to present his/her work to the community as a representative of the program	Structure and supervise closely; Communicate successes to assistant principal and home; Give verbal praise; Link to behavioral plan at school and home; Offer frequent breaks	ABA teacher, classroom or special education teachers; Child-specific aide; Assistant principal; Parent/guardian
Physical or health impairment	Modify physical participation or reduce time spent in activities, according to individual needs; Offer greater role in bike design or in media presentation	Ensure accessibility for those with mobility impairments; Consider a fixed location, such as at a particular work bench; reduce physical activities	Child-specific aide to learn of special needs; Other specialists according to particular student situation; Parent/guardian
Sensory impairment: Blindness	Let student decide what repair/physical tasks he or she is comfortable with; Offer position in bike	Pair with a buddy; Position out of high-traffic zones, clear away obstructions; Do not allow use of	Child-specific aide; Classroom or special education teachers; Parent/guardian

(Continued)

(Continued)

Disability	Modified Service	Tips	Consult or collaborate with:
	design or media presentation if preferred; Oral presentation of ideas	potentially dangerous cleaning fluids	
Sensory impairment Deafness	Modify assessments as needed; Allow student to work individually to research information on bicycling if work area noise is too confusing; Offer opportunity to be part of media presentation for members of the deaf community	Accompany directions with signs; Develop safety provisions and emergency signals; Always secure student's attention before presenting information; Do not turn away from student when presenting information; inform staff of student communication needs	Child-specific aide; Classroom or special education teachers; Parent/guardian

References

Bybee, R.W., Buchwald, C.E., Crissman, S., Heil, D.R., Kuerbis, P.J., Matsumoto, C., et al. (1990). *Science and technology for the middle years: Frameworks for curriculum and instruction.* Washington, DC: National Center for Improving Science Education.

Dahir, C.A., & Stone, C.B. (2003). Accountability: A M.E.A.S.U.R.E. of the impact school counselors have on student achievement. *Professional School Counseling, 6*(3), 214–222.

Dewey, J. (1938). *Experience and education.* New York: Collier.

Elias, M.J., Zins, J.E., Weissberg, R.P., Frey, K.S., Greenberg, M.T., Haynes, N.M., et al. (1997). *Promoting social and emotional learning: Guidelines for educators.* Alexandra, VA: Association for Supervision and Curriculum Development (ASCD).

Eyler, J., & Giles, D.E. (1999). *Where's the learning in service learning?* San Francisco, CA: Jossey-Bass.

Gardner, H. (1993). *Frames of mind: The theory of multiple intelligences.* New York: Basic Books.

Gore, A. (2006). *An inconvenient truth.* New York: Rodale Press.

Hansen, J. (2004). A common-sense solution to global warming. *NPQ: New Perspectives Quarterly, 21*(4), 111–113.

Henderson, N., & Milstein, M.M. (2002). *Resiliency in schools: Making it happen for students and educators.* Thousand Oaks, CA: SAGE Publications.

Kahn, B.B. (2000). A model of solution-focused consultation for school counselors. *Professional School Counseling, 3*(4), 248–255.

Kolb, D.A. (1984). *Experiential learning: Experience as the source of learning and development.* Englewood Cliffs, NJ: Prentice-Hall.

Lieberman, G.A., & Hoody, L.L. (1998). *Closing the achievement gap: Using the environment as an integrating context for learning.* Executive summary—State education and environmental roundtable. San Diego, CA. Retrieved April 24, 2006, from http://www.eric.ed.gov/ERICDocs/data/ericdocs2/content_storage_01/0000000b/80/11/67/20.pdf.

Madigan, P. (2000). *The environmental service-learning research project.* Washington, DC: Corporation for National Service. Retrieved July 26, 2006, from http://www.nationalserviceresources.org/filemanager/download/NatlServFellows/madigan.pdf.

Massachusetts Department of Education. (1999). *Character, civility, and the Massachusetts curriculum frameworks.* Malden, MA: Author.

Massachusetts Department of Education. (2000). *Mathematics curriculum framework.* Retrieved November 25, 2005, from http://www.doe.mass.edu/frameworks/math/2000/final.doc.

Massachusetts Department of Education. (2001a). *English language arts curriculum framework.* Retrieved November 25, 2005, from http://www.doe.mass.edu/frameworks/ela/0601.pdf.

Massachusetts Department of Education. (2001b). *Science and technology/engineering curriculum framework.* Retrieved November 25, 2005, from http://www.doe.mass.edu/frameworks/scitech/2001/0501.doc.

Massachusetts Department of Education. (2003). *History and social science curriculum framework.* Retrieved November 25, 2005, from http://www.doe.mass.edu/frameworks/hss/final.doc.

Massachusetts Department of Education. (2004). *Mathematics curriculum framework.* Retrieved August 10, 2006, from http://www.doe.mass.edu/frameworks/math/052504_sup.pdf.

Massachusetts Department of Education. (2005a). *Student support, career, & education services.* Retrieved August 10, 2006, from http://www.doe.mass.edu/ssce/.

Massachusetts Department of Education. (2005b). *Career development.* Retrieved November 25, 2005, from http://www.doe.mass.edu/cd/.

Massachusetts Department of Education. (2006). *Science and technology/engineering curriculum framework.* Retrieved August 10, 2006, from http://www.doe.mass.edu/frameworks/scitech/0106standards.pdf.

Metcalf, L. (1995). *Counseling toward solutions: A practical solution-focused program for working with students, teachers, and parents.* San Francisco, CA: Jossey-Bass.

Mitchell, J.F.B., Loew, J., Wood, R.A., & Vellinga, M. (2006). Extreme events due to human-induced climate change. *Philosophical Transactions: Mathematical, Physical & Engineering Sciences, 364,* 2117–2133.

Muir, J. (1988). *My first summer in the sierra.* San Francisco, CA: Sierra Club Books.

Muscott, H.S. (2000). A review and analysis of service-learning programs involving students with emotional/behavioral disorders. *Education and Treatment of Children, 23*(3), 346–368.

Oppenheimer, M. (1998). Global warming and the stability of the west Antarctic ice sheet. *Nature, 393,* 325–332.

Reschly, D.J., & Yessldyke, J.E. (2002). Paradigm shift: The past is not the future. In A. Thomas & J. Grimes (Eds.), *Best practices in school psychology–IV* (pp. 3–20). Washington, DC: National Association of School Psychologists.

Saltmarsh, J. (1997). Ethics, reflection, purpose, and compassion: Community service learning. *New Directions for Student Services, 77,* 81–93.

Schine, J., Shoup, B., & Harrington, D. (1981). *New roles for early adolescents.* New York: The National Commission on Resources for Youth.

Schon, D.A. (1983). *The reflective practitioner: How professionals think in action.* New York: Basic Books.

Schukar, R. (1997). Enhancing the middle school curriculum through service learning. *Theory into Practice, 36*(3), 176–183.

Search Institute. (2000). *An asset builder's guide to service-learning.* Minneapolis, MN: Author.

Shepard, J.S. (2004). Multiple ways of knowing: Fostering resiliency through providing opportunities for participating in learning. *Reclaiming Children and Youth, 12*(4), 210–216.

Sklare, G.B. (2005). *Brief counseling that works: A solution-focused approach for school counselors and administrators.* Thousand Oaks, CA: Corwin Press.

Stone, C.B., & Dahir, C.A. (2006). *The transformed school counselor.* Boston, MA: Lahaska Press.

Section IV
Service-Learning Print and Internet Resources

The following print and web listings are a small sampling of resources that we found useful for service-learning project ideas and implementation strategies. Most of the websites include links to other service-learning resources. Note that this is not meant to be an exhaustive list.

Annotated Bibliography

Association for Supervision and Curriculum Development. (2001). *Character education/service-learning*. Alexandria, VA: Author.
    This publication includes full text journal articles, book excerpts, Internet resources, and annotated bibliographies on service-learning and character education.

Cairn, R.W., & Kielsmeier, J.C. (Eds.) (1995). *Growing hope: A sourcebook on integrating youth service into the school curriculum*. Roseville, MN: National Youth Leadership Council.
    Considered the first service-learning guidebook, the volume contains hands-on ideas, sample program materials, implementation techniques, and resource contacts for K-12 service-learning projects.

Chadwick, K.G. (2004). *Improving schools through community engagement: A practical guide for educators*. Thousand Oaks, CA: Corwin.
    The book provides a framework that can be used in designing and implementing initiatives to more effectively engage the community in K-12 education.

Education Commission of the States. (2001). *Service-learning and standards tool kit*. Denver, CO: Author.
    This tool kit links service-learning with standards-based educational reform. It provides a rationale and policy implications for service-learning as well as samples of service-learning curricula and projects, methods of assessment, lists of resources, and useful worksheets linking curriculum with assessment.

Education Commission of the States. (2002). *Learning that lasts: How service-learning can become an integral part of schools, states, and communities*. Denver, CO: Author.
    This publication addresses questions about institutionalizing service-learning. It explores how leaders at the state and local levels have developed long-term, large-scale systems that support and sustain service-learning.

Education Commission of the States. (2003). *Making the case for social and emotional learning and service-learning.* Denver, CO: Author.

This brief provides an overview and description of both social–emotional learning and service-learning as tools to improve the lives and academic performance of students. It describes how the two practices are interrelated and the research evidence that supports its expanded use in schools.

Gulati-Partee, G., & Finger, W.R. (1996). *Critical issues in K-12 service-learning.* Raleigh, NC: National Society for Experiential Education.

Each chapter of this volume presents the experiences of professionals addressing a particular issue or challenge in implementing service-learning. The authors discuss successful strategies to overcome challenges and also reflect on barriers to implementation that they were not successful in overcoming.

Kaye, C.B. (2003). *The complete guide to service-learning: Proven, practical ways to engage students in civic responsibility, academic curriculum, and social action.* Minneapolis, MN: Free Spirit Publishing.

This book offers ideas, activities, reflections, and recommendations for service-learning programs from a former classroom teacher. It places service-learning in a curricular context that explains its importance, essential elements, and addresses challenges.

Lewis, B.A. (1995). *The kid's guide to service projects.* Minneapolis, MN: Free Spirit Publishing.

The book contains over 500 ideas for service projects for students in grades K-12. Project possibilities range from simple ideas that can be implemented by a single person to large-scale projects that involve entire communities.

Maryland Student Service Alliance. (1993). *Service-learning and special education guide.* Maryland State Department of Education: Author.

This instructional manual provides guidance for engaging students with disabilities in service-learning. It includes suggestions for inclusion, evaluation, and working with the community.

National Youth Leadership Council. (2004–2006). *Growing to greatness: The state of service-learning project.* St. Paul, MN: Author.

This set of three reports documents the unfolding story of service-learning, summarizing evidence of the personal, social, career, and academic benefits. It also provides useful information about implementation and public policies issues. There are descriptions of the many ways that students contribute to the community through service-learning.

RMC Research Corporation. (2003). *Connecting thinking and action: Ideas for service-learning reflection.* Denver, CO: RMC Research Corporation.

This guide addresses reflection, a necessary component of service-learning programs. It provides ideas for a variety of reflection activities, templates to copy, a brief summary of research and theory on reflection, and resources for more ideas.

Search Institute. (2000). *An asset builder's guide to service-learning.* Minneapolis, MN: Author.

The guide assists in developing strategies for doing service-learning in ways that maximize its potential to build developmental assets.

Wisconsin Department of Public Instruction. *Learning from experience: A collection of service-learning projects linking academic standards to curriculum.* Madison, WI: Author.

This publication presents examples of successful service-learning projects as described by teachers across the state of Wisconsin.

Service-Learning Internet Resources

Constitutional Rights Foundation

www.crf-usa.org: Constitutional Rights Foundation offers a broad range of service-learning resources.

Council for Service-Learning Excellence

www.nslexchange.org: Council for Service-Learning Excellence, under the auspices of the National Youth Leadership Council, offers technical assistance and professional development opportunities. It also operates the National Service-Learning Exchange, where staff answer questions about service learning or connect you with peer mentors.

Education Commission of the States

www.ecs.org: Education Commission of the States (ECS) is an interstate agency providing regional, state, and national service-learning policy information.

Institute for Global Education and Service Learning

www.igesl.org: Institute for Global Education and Service Learning (IGESL) provides many tools for service-learning implementation, such as facilitators' guidebooks and student portfolios.

Learn and Serve America

www.learnandserve.org: Learn and Serve America, a program of the Corporation for National and Community Service (www.nationalservice.org/), provides grants and scholarships to schools, colleges, and nonprofit groups that participate in community service programs.

Learning in Deed

www.learningindeed.org: Learning in Deed was established to broaden the use of service learning in school districts across America and promotes service learning as a means of engaging youth in a powerful way in their learning and in their communities.

National Center for Learning and Citizenship

www.ecs.org/nclc: The National Center for Learning and Citizenship, established by the Education Commission of the States, works with state and district administrators and educators and promotes service-learning opportunities in K-12 education.

National Indian Youth Leadership Project

www.niylp.org: The National Indian Youth Leadership Project provides service-learning resources for tribes, Native American youth, and tribal schools.

National Service Inclusion Project

www.serviceandinclusion.org: The National Service Inclusion Project, a Corporation for National and Community Service training and technical assistance provider, works to ensure that *everyone* has the opportunities to serve. It provides assistance on the inclusion of individuals with disabilities in service programs.

National Service-Learning Clearinghouse (NSLC)

www.servicelearning.org: National Service-Learning Clearinghouse (NSCL) is program of Learn and Serve America, which operates a website supporting the service-learning efforts of schools, higher education institutions, communities, and tribal nations. The site offers timely information, thousands of free online resources, a library of service-learning materials, national service-learning listservs, as well as reference and technical assistance services.

National Youth Leadership Council

www.nylc.org: National Youth Leadership Council (NYCL) supports service learning as a movement linking youths, educators, and communities to redefine the roles of young people in society.

Points of Light Foundation

www.pointsoflight.org: The Points of Light Foundation provides access to a national network of volunteer centers, and information on service learning from a community-based organization's perspective.

RMC Research Corporation, Denver

www.rmcdenver.com: RMC is a national research corporation. Service learning is an area of expertise at RMC's Denver office. As a national leader in supporting the positive development of youth, RMC Denver provides a wide range of projects, products, and services that support service-learning.

Service-Learning Partnership

www.servicelearningpartnership.org: The Service-Learning Partnership is an organization that advocates for service-learning funding and legislation.

Search Institute

www.search-institute.org: The Search Institute is a nonprofit organization whose mission is to provide leadership, knowledge, and resources to promote healthy children, youth, and communities. At the center of the Institute's work is the framework of *40 Developmental Assets*, which are positive experiences and personal qualities that young people need to grow up healthy, caring, and responsible.

State Education Agency Network

www.seanetonline.org: State Education Agency Network (SEANet) provides leadership for statewide K-12 service-learning initiatives. A downloadable listing of each state's service-learning website addresses is available. There is also a link for a Learn and Service application and funding instructions.

Youth Service America

www.ysa.org: The Youth Service America website offers free curriculum guides and searches volunteer opportunities by zip code.

There are many other valuable websites produced by individual state departments of education that list local service-learning resources. In addition, there are several national listservs. To join, go to the NSLC website (www.servicelearning.org), click on "Resources," then "Listservs and Newsletters" for instructions.

Epilogue

Urgent challenges confront our schools and communities. In this time of budget cuts and high stakes testing, schools are forced to make difficult choices in curricular and personnel matters. Students also face unparalleled demands to achieve academically, work collaboratively, maintain good interpersonal relationships, avoid negative peer pressure, make responsible choices, manage emotional responses, and contribute to their community. Throughout this book, we have presented service learning as a sound practice for meeting those challenges.

Service learning brings students' "heads" and "hearts" together. In so doing, it integrally links the work of teachers and mental health professionals in promoting positive youth development. Because service learning is an authentic context for teaching and learning, it contributes to key academic achievement and career development goals, and, at the same time, fosters students' social and emotional growth. Added benefits are an improved school climate and community support.

Service learning is a change in philosophy about how teachers and mental health professionals view youth. It requires that we recognize the students' capacities to address many unmet needs in the community. Instead of viewing students as the problem, as deficient or passive recipients of education, service learning suggests that we view students as part of the solution— as competent and capable contributors to their community. School psychologists and counselors need to help provide opportunities for students to be resources.

There is a caution: Service learning is not a panacea for many of the ills afflicting the nation's students, schools, and communities. It is important for school personnel to be critical consumers of these claims. In particular, we need to remind ourselves that student and school problems are extremely complex, and no single educational program could possibly address all of them.

Although service learning is not a cure-all, research tells us that it is more than just a promising practice. By incorporating service learning into your work, you will begin to understand how much it has to offer—as an authentic intervention for social, emotional, career, and academic growth. Ultimately, service learning has the potential to transform young people from passive recipients of information to agents of social change.

Chances are you became a school psychologist or school counselor because you cared about youth and wanted to make a difference. It is hard to make a more profound difference than that which you can achieve through service learning. As children's advocate Marian Wright Edelman put it, "A lot of people are waiting for Martin Luther King or Mahatma Gandhi to come back—but they are gone. We are it. It is up to us. It is up to you."

Subject Index

About the Authors

Felicia L. Wilczenski, Ed.D., is Professor and Chair of the Department of Counseling and School Psychology at the University of Massachusetts Boston. She teaches in both the school psychology and school counseling programs. Professor Wilczenski's work focuses on service-learning applications in graduate education and in K-12 settings. Her research explores the process and outcomes of service-learning interventions.

Susan M. Coomey, M.Ed., C.A.G.S., is a graduate of the University of Massachusetts Boston and is licensed and nationally certified school psychologist in the Wachusett Regional School District in Holden Massachusetts. She has implemented and coordinated service learning at the middle and high school levels. Her professional interests are in service-learning interventions for students with special needs.

Printed in the United States
71954LV00002B/184-225